THE LAST OF

THE WAR BRIDES

Autobiography of Jacqueline O'Neill Dahm

The Nazis had an idea of how to win the Second World War; bomb the living hell out of the English civilian population until they had no spirit, nor resistance left. It simply did not work. The German high command hadn't counted on the British sense of humour coupled with their remarkable backbone.

Jacqueline O'Neill Dahm, standing a full four feet ten inches in her painted on stocking feet was just another Blitzed-Brit. At the end of hostilities she thought she had been served enough adversity for one lifetime. However, that changed when she married a Canadian soldier and promptly landed up on the wind and snow-swept prairies of Alberta.

Note for Librarians: A cataloguing record for this book is available from Library and Archives Canada at www.collectionscanada.ca/amicus/index-e.html
ISBN 1-4120-4724-2

Printed in Victoria, BC, Canada. Printed on paper with minimum 30% recycled fibre. Trafford's print shop runs on "green energy" from solar, wind and other environmentally-friendly power sources.

TRAFFORD
PUBLISHING™

Offices in Canada, USA, Ireland and UK

This book was published *on-demand* in cooperation with Trafford Publishing. On-demand publishing is a unique process and service of making a book available for retail sale to the public taking advantage of on-demand manufacturing and Internet marketing. On-demand publishing includes promotions, retail sales, manufacturing, order fulfilment, accounting and collecting royalties on behalf of the author.

Book sales for North America and international:
Trafford Publishing, 6E–2333 Government St.,
Victoria, BC v8t 4p4 CANADA
phone 250 383 6864 (toll-free 1 888 232 4444)
fax 250 383 6804; email to orders@trafford.com
Book sales in Europe:
Trafford Publishing (uk) Limited, 9 Park End Street, 2nd Floor
Oxford, UK ox1 1hh UNITED KINGDOM
phone 44 (0)1865 722 113 (local rate 0845 230 9601)
facsimile 44 (0)1865 722 868; info.uk@trafford.com
Order online at:
trafford.com/04-2532

10 9 8 7 6

DEDICATION

This book is dedicated to the memory of my father John Aloysius O'Neill, an Irishman by birth and a wanderer by nature. Father was a song and dance man in the early days of vaudeville in the United States of America. He was a gifted performer who, like so many of his colleagues, lacked even the rudiments of business acumen. As a result, his entire life was spent dancing a few steps ahead of utter bankruptcy. When he ultimately returned to England, to a second marriage, he became what we now call, a door-to-door salesman, a situation barely better than his song and dance career. Living impecuniously with father, after his wife, my mother, left for greener fields, taught me the fine art of survival and flexibility.

Wyoming Red
by *John Aloysius O'Neill*

Out of the badlands came Wyoming Red,
A much wanted man with a price on his head.
He rode through the town of Omega like hell,
After robbing the bank, and the saloon as well.
Old Sheriff Random was hot on his trail,
He said he'd bring the skunk in without fail.
The citizens cheered as he rode out of town,
Saying: "Shoot the cuss down, Sheriff,
Shoot the man down."

Now the cleverest hombre oft rides to a fall,
And the last laugh is always the best one of all.
Two hours later, the bad man – he saw,
The Killer shot first, being fast on the draw.
The Sheriff sidestepped … gave Red a surprise,
Then put a big slug between his two eyes.
The coyotes ran, yowling away from the sound,
"Shoot the cuss down, Sheriff,
Shoot the man down."

ACKNOWLEDGEMENTS

A long time ago I came across something that the French born Quaker Minister, Stephen Grellet (1773-1855) said: "I expect to pass through this world but once. Any good thing, therefore, that I can do or any kindness I can show to any fellow human being let me do it now. Let me not defer nor neglect it, for I shall not pass this way again."

As I read the passage, it struck me that it somehow reflected my own philosophy on life, which is: "I will do my best to find kind words for my fellow beings, even if they are not in turn friendly towards me."

Fortunately, my days have mostly been filled with those who have gone out of their way to enrich my life with their goodness. Through their very being they have all made this book possible. My husband Allan, whose inner strength fought off all manner of adversities that afflicted him, showing me how to better cope with life. My children, Muff-Anne, Janine, Timmie and Christopher, each with their completely different approaches to life, each with their own special love.

And finally, I must express my sincere thanks to Valerie Humphreys and her partner George Matheson for their 'beyond the call of duty' kindness and advice in putting my book together.

To A Friend
by *Jacqueline O'Neill*

You're always there to cheer my way,
Whenever I am blue.
And when I've had a tedious day,
I always turn to you.

For you will always lend a hand,
And soothe my troubled mind.
You make this place a better land,
For you're so sweet and kind.

I know you'll never turn away,
If I seek your advice.
You're always just too glad to stay,
No need to ask you twice.

I want to thank you, dearest friend,
For every little thing.
While I have you for my friend,
I'm richer than a king.

Chapter 1

Of Nuns and Such

I was born in London, England, in the last part of the first quarter of the twentieth century. I was born in a charity ward of a hospital in the district of Marylebone, properly speaking this area is Mary-le-bone, but no Londoner calls it that, it is always shortened to 'Marryben'.

The family consisted of my father John Aloysius O'Neill, mother Margaret Helen, myself, and my sister Mamie, a few years older than I who had been.born a twin, but her brother had died at birth. We lived in a poor area of Notting Hill Gate on the third floor of a three-storey house. Our living quarters consisted of two rooms, with a gas stove on the landing for our cooking needs. A cupboard on the landing contained our dishes and pots and pans. A fair-sized enamel basin served for washing the dishes. It stood on an old-fashioned divided wooden apple box upended. The washing soda, etcetera were stored on the shelf inside. One of the rooms was living-dining also bedroom for Mamie and I. We took turns with a chair-bedstead and a sofa for sleeping. The sofa was much more comfortable. Mostly I got the chair-bedstead. The other room was my parents' bedroom. The only running water was a cold water tap on the next landing down. So we kept two or three galvanized buckets of water upstairs - covering them with an odd assortment of lids - thus cutting down on the trips downstairs. There was also a toilet on this landing, a toilet, but no wash basin therein! Building codes of today would certainly condemn such facilities. As to a bathtub, I don't know if any of the other 'flats' had such a luxury! We received our 'Saturday night dipping' in a galvanized tub!!

My earliest memory is of a neighbour lady giving me three red roses on my third birthday, some would say that

I can't remember back that far, but I do.

The London of my childhood was the London of the lamplighters, the Punch and Judy shows, the street criers, and the buskers – whose presence filled the street with exciting and sometimes mysterious sounds. Those things I remember from long ago. There were the rag and bone men that came around crying, "rags, bones, bottles, sacks." One very unusual street vendor came around with vinegar and salt and had the strangest sing-song cry, he would call out, "Penny a pint of vinaigar, salt penny a lump," and we thought what a very strange way to make a living, and it certainly was. Another street crier used to shout, "Par elarkiah," or so it sounded to us. Whatever he was selling I didn't know then and I still don't know. There was a chap with a little horse and cart that had a miniature merry-go-round on it and for a small jam jar, we could get a short ride on the merry-go-round or a larger jam jar gave us a longer ride, and that was always fun for us. In those days we could get a ha'penny for a small jam jar and a penny for a large one.

Night time was very different from now; I can remember candles, candlesticks, oil lamps, and gas mantles from the days of my childhood.

I recall my father attempting to light the gas mantle and trying to be very careful, but inevitably it would break, so it would be another tuppence or tuppence ha'penny for a new mantle, an added expense we could have done without. At times like that he would say something in Gaelic so my sister and I wouldn't know he was using bad words, but on one occasion we did hear him say "Damn and blast it all to hell!"

Muffin men and hot cross bun men selling their wares around the streets of London in those days often came to our district. On Sunday mornings; a girl with a beautiful voice used to sing on the streets for money and sometimes we might be given a penny by father to throw to her. On those occasions we felt very glad.

I shall never forget the lady who was dressed in long black clothes, who used to sweep a crossing in Ladbroke

Grove with an old fashioned 'witches broom' of twigs. Mamie and I thought she was a witch!! Probably though - just a pensioner augmenting her income with the pennies passersby would give her.

As a young man my father had spent over twenty years in the United States of America. He was married there when he was nineteen, but his wife died after only two years of marriage. He stayed on in the States for quite a while and earned his living as a vaudevillian, a song and dance man.

Savannah
by *John Aloysius O'Neill*

When I was boy, I used to long,
To be a soldier; brave, and strong.
To roam the seas like Captain Kidd,
And bring home treasure, like he did.
Then one day, my dream came true,
I joined the Navy, and the Boys in Blue.
I've sailed the seas to every land,
Now I'm homing back to Dixieland.
I'm going back to old Savannah,
The place where I belong.

Where moonbeams streak across the cotton fields,
And nightingales trill their song.
You can hear the darkies singing,
Round the campfires burning low.
So I'm going back to old Savannah,
It's the best old place I know.

When he returned to England, he did a little vaudeville work but I think by that time it may have been dying out. So, he started to do painting and decorating of houses. He felt fortunate to have found this job, for at that time, many employers advertising for help would add a footnote "No Irish or Catholics need apply." He did this until he had a very bad accident on the job and was in hospital for quite a while. After that he was no longer able to continue the decorating and because of the existing prejudices it was hard for him to get work of any kind. So he started to sell things from door-to-door and some days he would take me with him. Often we would return home after selling very little. It seemed to me that we had walked for miles and miles in vain.

My father was quite a few years older than my mother, his second wife, and I can't say that I ever knew much about her. She had very heavy black hair and brilliant green eyes. She was a very cold person and I can't remember her ever hugging my sister or I or ever saying, "I love you." I don't think she did, because she would soon leave us. My mother left my father once or twice and took Mamie and I around seaside towns, to sell things as my father did, to make a living for us. I don't know how long we wandered about with her; it was always in places by the sea - Benfleet, Canvey Island, Margate, Ramsgate, Southend-on-Sea. We never knew where we were going to spend the night, or if we were going to spend the night under shelter or out in the open, but eventually we did return home to my father. How long she stayed with us I don't remember, but she finally did leave us for good and we have never seen her since. I was five years old.

My Last Romance
by *John Aloysius O'Neill*

Summer days, and skies of blue,
By the sea, where I met you.
Where we sat, or roamed the sand,
Happy lovers, hand in hand.
You whispered, "Dear, I love you only."
Truth shone in your eyes of blue.
Now you've left me sad and lonely,
All my dreams have gone with you.

I thought our love would last forever,
You swore to me your heart was mine.
I thought that naught in life could sever,
Love like ours, so pure and fine.
When you gave me back my token,
Told me sadly, we must part,
All your vows to me were broken,
Like my dreams, just like my heart.

It was at that time that my father's accident landed him in hospital. There were no relations or anyone close who would take us in for a while. Neighbours took us in for a few days but then we were sent to St. Joseph's Convent just outside London, and there began a lot of things I would rather not remember. I suppose that both my sister and I knew that we were different from most kids and I imagine we dealt with it in different ways. Mamie, as I said, was a few years older than I, she put on a brave front and rebelled, well, as much as you could rebel in a convent! I suppose I was so bewildered by what happened I just tried to obey all the rules, even though the nuns were very, very strict. Some would even say they were very harsh.

I think their Order was of the Sacred Heart and to this day I can still remember a few of the nuns. Mother Superior, her name was Sister Mary Henry, she was a very large woman and very, very, strict; Sister Mary Raymond, also a very large woman and very strict. I think they thought they were doing their duty, but it was not a good experience for us there. I don't wish to say anything against them because I think maybe they thought this was the way they had to bring up children, but our time was not happy. There was a young nun, Sister Mary Audrey, and I think we all liked her because she was always so kind and she was pretty too. An elderly nun, Sister Mary Augustine, who was very pleasant, played kindergarten games with all us younger children. If I can say one nice thing for the convent it would be that they did teach us to speak properly, and I'm glad of that.

We were all allotted clothes with a number on, my number was number 16, my sister's was 31, and we were given a clean bundle of clothes every week with these numbers on them. We slept in very large dormitories and had our numbers on our beds. I cannot remember any of the names or the numbers of the girls who slept on either side of me and my sister was not in the same dormitory.

I must tell you of Sister Mary Cuthbert. She was a Cockney, and getting along in years, and if we misbehaved she always chased you holding a 'plimsoll', which is what they used to call runners in England, maybe they call them runners now. Many was the time that my sister Mamie would get threatened with the plimsoll and Sister Mary Cuthbert would shout, "Mamie MacNeill, come 'ere". Our name was O'Neill, but to Sister Mary it was always, "Mamie MacNeill". Fortunately, she could rarely catch Mamie and even if she did, she wouldn't do much with the plimsoll, just scold. But I do know my sister had to spend many a time in a closet because she did rebel and I suppose with good reason. Certainly not on Sister Mary Cuthbert's orders!

One or two teachers came to the convent from the outside, including Miss Green who taught art and we quite liked her. There was also a Miss O'Connell who was quite pleasant and a Miss Glockner, not a very popular teacher.

I can still picture her in my mind, she was a cripple and walked with a cane and I don't ever remember seeing her smile. I imagine we were all a little in awe of her. All the nuns lived in the convent.

I think we must have been awakened around five o'clock each morning because we always marched off to six o'clock Mass, whatever the weather whatever the season. We didn't have breakfast before we left for Mass. Our breakfast when we did get it, consisted of very watery porridge or for a change porridge like cement and we may have had some skim milk. The convent food was not exciting, to say the least. We looked forward to a dessert on Sundays of prunes and a very thin custard. Sometimes for dessert we had what we called semolina and that was cream of wheat. I think it was made with water and had thick cinnamon sticks in it and very little sugar and there were always very heavy skins on it. To this day I hate cinnamon. We always said Grace before and after meals, in spite of what we received.

After breakfast there would be a few minutes of exercise in the hall and then a little recreation time before the start of lessons. We would stop schooling around eleven o'clock and then we would have compulsory chores to do, sweeping, dusting, oiling the heavy wooden floors and various other equally unappealing activities.

At twelve o'clock noon the Angelus would ring. No matter where you were at this time you had to kneel and say the Angelus, even if you were outside on gravel or cement you still had to do this. We all developed a kind of squatting position, 'twas much easier on the knees! After the Angelus it was time for a delightful lunch of either very watery soup with hard crusts or a sandwich made with very hard bread and maybe some skim milk to drink. There was no dessert at lunch time. After we had finished lunch we helped to clear away the tables and then we went back to lessons. I must say I really did enjoy the lessons. To this day I still like to learn new things. When afternoon lessons were through we were allowed to play in the playground for a while before supper time.

If it was a Friday, of course we would have fish, macaroni and cheese on Wednesdays, or vice-versa for a change. I cannot remember ever having roast beef, roast pork, roast lamb, and certainly we didn't have steaks and chops. One particular delight was steak and kidney pudding and sometimes the crust was quite raw in the middle, so that really was quite ugly. We were given stew, which looked very much like the beef stew that I serve to my dogs today. Sometimes there would be ground meat or fish croquettes; none of the menus were very appetizing.

In winter we were allowed some playtime in the hall after the evening meal, and if it was summer we could play outside, but it was always under the nuns' supervision. A little before it was time to get ready for bed one of the nuns would bring a big basket full of hard crusts which had margarine on them and this was our before going to bed treat. We weren't given anything to drink with these crusts, although if you wanted, you could get a drink of water afterwards.

We had to kneel by our beds for the evening prayers and they were quite long. There was always a Litany or two and many other prayers besides, and I must say, I did not like the church or praying when I was little. It was too tiring and there seemed to be too much of it. I especially recall Sister Mary Cuthbert reciting Litanies with her 'Ouse of David and H'Ark of the Covenant'. After prayers we were not allowed to talk to one another and if we did we were made to stand by our beds for a while as punishment.

In every dormitory there was a cubicle where the nun slept and as little girls will, we always wondered what the nuns would look like without their wimples on, and we wondered if they wore nighties like we did, but I don't think I ever got to see one.

Some girls' stay at the convent was paid for by parents or guardians and it wasn't too hard to determine which girls' room and board was paid. It was their manner, the way they seemed to look down on the girls who were not sponsored. For example, two sisters, Cynthia and Pauline - if any of us 'lesser girls' should touch them

14

accidentally they would take an imaginary brush and brush the contamination from their clothes and blow it off. I heartily dislike the names of Cynthia and Pauline because I always associate them with those two girls. Now this is rather silly I suppose, but it's something I can't help.

There were some rather sad girls living at the convent, including Ida Spider - I don't know if that was her real name. She was mentally fragile and she wasn't expected to do any work or any lessons because she was not able. She would sit at her desk with two fingers in her mouth just moving her head from side to side hour after hour. Then there was Pat, sadly she had no hair - I think she lost it when she got alopecia. There was a girl there with only one arm, how she lost her arm I never did know, maybe it was a birth defect. Her name was Kathleen.

In a lighter vein I remember May. She would ask to be excused from the class and someone would find her swinging from the roller towels in the outside toilet facilities. If the teacher taking that class was a nun, she would ask another girl to go and bring May back to class and May, poor soul, would be made to stand in the corner for a while.

Occasionally we were taken out by the nuns for a walk on a Sunday. One particular Sunday I remember very well. I asked one of the nuns in charge if I might go to the bathroom. She told me that I must wait until I got back to the convent. I had an accident and was made to feel my shame in front of the whole group. When we got back to the convent, this nun took me to the Mother Superior and I can remember hearing her words, "You bold beast, what do you have to say for yourself?" I thought I must be the most terrible sinner in the world, the lowest of the low. I was five years old!

In our dormitory early in the mornings on Saturdays, one of the nuns would bring us a chipped enamel bowl full of senna tea. It was always very strong, a very nasty ugly brown liquid, and whether we needed it or not, we were made to take this laxative. One Saturday during the senna tea procedure the nun was called away for a few minutes.

In our dormitory there was a row of pigeon holes where we kept our clothes and any small treasure we might have. Behind the pigeon holes there was a row of holes about the size of an old fashioned penny. I quickly poured the contents of my mug down one of these. Of course I had no idea where this would end up, perhaps in some never-never-land. Imagine my horror some time later, when one of the very large formidable nuns delivered this message to all in our dormitory, "Woe betide the wicked girl who is responsible for such willful damage to property, she will have to answer to me." We all knew what that meant, she had a very large stick, and she used it on us quite often. I made up my mind then to only admit I was guilty if she blamed someone else but to my great relief she never did.

As you can imagine our clothes were very plain. We were all dressed the same but it seemed to me some of the more fortunate girls like Cynthia and Pauline always looked a little better in their clothes than we did. I really thought we looked like poor orphans. Our clothes consisted of a white chemise, navy blue bloomers, a navy blue woollen sweater, a navy blue skirt and a navy blue pinafore. The pinafore had some white polka dots on it. In the summer, instead of the navy blue sweater, we were given a dark blouse to wear. I don't think we had any special skirt for the summer, just a lighter blouse, black stockings and boots.

Not a day went by when we weren't lectured on the sins of vanity and pride. No one was allowed to wear bracelets, necklaces, or rings, and if one had long hair that needed to be tied back, they had to tie it back with string, no ribbons were allowed. We were lectured daily on the dangers of impure thoughts and words. There was a general feeling among us that if we ever said 'bum' we would go straight to hell.

In those days we thought that nuns and priests weren't human and their word was absolute gospel. There were no priests in residence in the convent, but they came every day to say Mass, and they did give us lectures, which we didn't like at all, and sometimes found quite frightening, when they would go on about the dangers of sin and bad company. Isn't it a good thing that as we grow older we realize that all religious are only human? My sister and I did try to run away once but we were hardly outside the gates of the convent when we were brought back.

Highlights in the generally dreary convent were few and far between. One stands out very clearly in my memory. It was a May day, the day for crowning Our Lady. I thought there must have been some mistake when I was told that I was chosen for this privilege. Some of the other girls had seen the linen room nun put some lovely clothes on my bed. Everything was white. There was a white dress, a white veil, a white flower band to go over the veil, there was a white slip, even white bloomers. There were white shoes and white socks. I think I might have felt like a princess that day.

There was a procession and hymns to Our Lady and then came the crowning of Our Lady. A small stepladder was placed at the foot of the statue of Our Lady; a nun stood nearby to steady the steps as I mounted them and placed a wreath of flowers on Our Lady's head. I remember feeling so proud and happy. I felt like a princess, quite sure that all the other girls wished they were me. Sadly, I was not allowed to keep my 'princess finery' on all day. As the festivities were over, I had to change back into my 'orphan' outfit.

One day that was looked forward to very much was 'visitors day,' which only came about once a month, usually on a Sunday. I think parents or friends had to get special permission if they wanted to visit any day other than Sunday, and as our father lived quite a way from the convent, he couldn't come to visit very often, and we had no other relatives.

When parents and visitors brought treats for the kids they were not allowed to take charge of them themselves but they had to be given over to a nun who took care of them and doled them out as she saw fit. When I recall this 'treaty' time as I call it behind my mind, I remember some of the girls were rather unmannerly, very forward, or just plain rude. If they had no treats of their own or if they had finished theirs they would go begging from the girls who did have treats and the cry was always the same, "Oh give me some, I know you're kind." Even at my young age, I knew this was very insincere and not the way to behave. Father had always taught my sister and I to be polite, not forward, always to listen.

One day father came to visit my sister and I on a week day. We knew that he must have something important to tell us as it was not a regular visiting day. He told us that he had been asking the authorities if he could take us from the convent. They told him that as there was no mother in the home and no woman to look after us they would not allow him as we were underage. But they did say we would be allowed short visits with him.

On our first visit with him we were very surprised to discover that he had moved from the home we shared together and rented a spacious housekeeping room in a house, owned by a Catholic family named Linstead. I think there were seven children in the family, including a girl my sister's age and a girl my age. So there was no problem in making sleeping arrangements for us. I think my father made this move hoping the authorities would let him take us from the convent permanently, but this was to be some time yet to come.

The times we spent with this family were very happy and we did enjoy their company. Mrs. Linstead felt it quite natural to cook for us as well as her own family and we were rather glad. Even though our Daddie tried to make nice meals, he wasn't the best cook in the world. That first visit ended all too soon and it was time to go back to the convent and Daddie said, "We'll be together again soon," and we were.

When we got back to the convent the nuns expressed the hope that my sister and I had behaved like young ladies. Their maxim was, "Little children should be seen, and not heard."

The girls wanted to know all about our time on the 'outside', so for a while we were quite the celebrities regaling little groups with stories of the singing and dancing of the Pearlies in the streets and how afterwards they would pass the hat around with some of the money they collected going to charities. I imagine they would have kept some of the money for keeping their outfits in good repair. In those days there really was a king and queen of the Pearlies. On the many occasions I have been back to England, I have never seen Pearlies and this is very sad if they are dying out, because they really were an historic institution.

Another story we shared with our fellow 'inmates' was of things we had seen and heard in Hyde Park at Speakers Corner. The chap they called Prince Monolulu seemed to be very well known to the public. I don't think he was really a prince. He was a six foot six African and certainly would have stood out in any crowd. He wore very brightly coloured robes, feathers and plumes and things and he would tell the public, "I gotta a horse, I gotta horse." So I guess he was a bookmaker. There were others at the corner who disagreed with what the government was doing about this problem or the other and those who didn't like this politician or that one. I suppose it was only really interesting to the public when the speakers got heckled from the crowd.

We told the girls how delighted we were with 'Elfin Oak' in Kensington Gardens, a very old oak tree with painted carvings of little gnomes, pixies and fairies. Even now, at this late stage in my life it is still a delight to visit the Elfin Oak.

The convent had a netball team, which in North America is called basketball. Some of the older girls were quite tall so, of course, they were on the team. There was always excitement in the air when they were going to play another school or a convent. The team was given Bovril to drink on these days, I suppose it was for extra strength for the play. Everyone in the convent was given this extra treat. If one of the netball games fell on a Friday they would be given Marmite, a veggie substitute for Bovril.

Christmas meant a lot of praying and church going and I truly believe that no child ever enjoys church. Too young to understand what is going on and too tiring for to sit still for so long. The nuns did serve us proper meat for dinner on Christmas Day and an orange and there was candy passed around, but it was only passed around once. Christmas was time for a concert and I think most of the kids enjoyed the affair, although it probably was quite dreadful. We all enjoyed the freedom from the tight surveillance, even for a little while.

I'm sure that all of the parents and visitors who came to the annual garden fête thought that the nuns were guardian angels and those that weren't were all mother figures. Nuns at the fête went around patting heads, lauding the merits of this wonderful child or that, making believe they were looking to see if all the kids had their lemonade and a cake, or a sandwich. Normally no nun ever patted heads. Nuns made no physical contact with you except maybe to pull or cuff your ear if you giggled in church. It was a fête with the Great Pretender scene. On these occasions there were many tables of crafts and other things for sale, and I must say, some of the nuns did do very well, and made quite a bit of money for the convent, and some of the girls there were quite clever with their crafts too. I can't say that I was among them. I do remember making a letter holder of grey silk and raffia and I was terribly proud of it.

The days in the convent seemed to be so very long. This may have been because the atmosphere was so barren and devoid of love. We had to make most of our own entertainment. In the asphalt playground there were horse chestnut trees growing, and in the autumn when the chestnuts would fall, we would make necklaces from them. We played a game with a conker on a string. Each girl would have a conker on a string and try to break the other one's conker. I don't know what we called the game, but we thought it was fun; maybe we called it 'conkers'? For anyone who doesn't know, we called the horse chestnuts "conkers". We played old fashioned cat's cradle – we had "raggies", little dolls that we made from bits of rag with beds made of old fashioned match boxes. My raggie was indeed very raggy. Some girls would keep a woolly bear in a match box and this would be their 'pet'. I don't know if you call them woolly bears here, they are caterpillars about two and a half inches long. I have never liked anything that wiggles, so I never had one of these 'pets'. It was strictly verboten to take those 'woolly bear pets' inside where they would be confiscated immediately. What fate they met with is not hard to imagine. There was always skipping, and every little girl was happy to master the double skipping rope game.

* * *

It was nearing fall and the days were drawing in, we looked forward to our second cheerless winter in the convent, but there was a bright spot on the horizon. One day in early December, Mamie and I were called in to the Mother Superior's office. Wondering what was in store for us there, we were not in any great hurry to get there.

"Come along look sharp, pick up your feet," said the nun guiding us there.

"Stand up straight," Mother Superior told us when we got there. "Hold your heads up." "Now then," she went on, "you will be allowed to spend Christmas week with your father, see that you behave yourselves, that's all, dismissed."

How we looked forward to the day when our father would come and get us. What a special week that was, full of happy times and happy memories. Every day there was something to look forward to.

The Linsteads made us part of their family in everything they did. Lydia, one of the Linstead girls, had a birthday party and we were invited. Mrs. Linstead made a very special birthday tea and everyone enjoyed it very much. We played many games and everyone was so very tired but a good time was had by all. The neighbour's children collected their party favours and went home. It was quite dark by then, and one of the older Linsteads went with them to see them home safely.

We attended a birthday party for Baby Jesus at the Linstead's church. I went with two of the younger Linstead

21

children. Mamie said she would stay and be with Angela. They liked to talk about poetry and books they had read, and they also liked to draw.

Everyone took part in decorating the Linstead's house for Christmas, and even the youngest of us got to stay up a little later that night. The tree was not decorated just yet, this was to be done on the morrow. There was holly, cedar boughs and mistletoe, and garlands of paper-chains that we had made, and the whole house was looking very gay indeed. As it was quite late when we went to bed, Irene didn't read us a story that night.

We were up early the next day looking forward to decorating the tree. We strung popcorn, we strung cranberries, and a few of the newspapers had instructions for making your own Christmas ornaments, so we made a few of those too. Mr. and Mrs. Linstead started to put gaily-wrapped parcels under the tree. In those days we had lighted candles for illumination on the Christmas tree but we didn't light any candles just then. I am sure the Fire Chiefs of today would be absolutely horrified at this practice! Another fun-filled day was coming to an end. Mrs. Linstead had made special treats for everyone, one of the boys played the piano and we sang carols and we had a fun supper of fish and chips and Irene promised a longer story tonight if everyone would hurry up and get ready for bed.

Christmas Eve and the Linstead home was a hive of activity. Neighbours dropping in and bringing gifts of goodwill. Everyone had their little jobs to do, putting nuts, fruit and candy in dishes, and getting the chestnuts ready for roasting. The pudding was already made and just about everything was ready for the big day and after a very hasty high tea it was time to get ready for the early evening Mass.

As we started out for the church, the air was crisp and soft snow was gently falling. When we got home after Mass, heads were counted to make sure that no one was left at the church, and it was agreed, after such an activity-filled day that no one would need any rocking to put them to sleep that night.

The following day, the big day, all the younger ones

among us were up at the crack of dawn, tiptoeing downstairs, trying to sound like mice, but I imagine we sounded more like bulls in a china shop, for it wasn't too long before the whole household was alive.

What a day of happy confusion that was. From early morn with everyone delightedly emptying their stockings 'til the last story was told at night around the fire's dying embers. Christmas in those days did not mean a mountain of very expensive gifts, and it did not mean going into debt to pay for Christmas, as is often the case nowadays, even with the average family. Many of the gifts were homemade and some came from Woolworths. Christmas meant sharing happy times with family and friends, and the meals we shared were a little more festive than our every day fare.

Boxing Day at the Linsteads, a little quieter day. It was still snowing outside, but not enough snow to make a snowman or make snowballs. Some of the older Linsteads were reading and a couple playing a board game but I think us younger ones were rather restless.

Later that day Angela asked, "Your Dad said he was going to tell us what it was like in America, do you think he will tell us after supper?"

"I think you should ask him and see what he says," said Mamie.

The favourite place for storytelling in the Linstead home was around the fire in the living room after high tea or supper. As he had promised to do, my Father regaled the Linsteads with stories about his life in America.

The entire household sat quiet, enraptured, as he told of his travels to the different states, his work in the music halls as a song and dance man and the interesting people he met on the circuit. Some of his cohorts, happy-go-lucky living only for the moment, some worried about their future, some quite sure that one day they were going to make it big, but sadly never did. But there were one or two who went on to make the big time, but most merely hoping for enough work just to pay their bills.

He told about riding the rails with his friend, George Harriman, how they hired themselves out as ranch hands in

Texas. Neither one of them knew anything about cattle and less about horses, they couldn't even ride one, and they were quickly and politely given the boot. They soon reasoned they might do better as door-to-door salesmen, but truly they did not have the heart for that kind of work.

They were part of a travelling medicine man show for a while. Always ready for a new experience, and a new challenge, and as neither one of them had anyone depending on them, and no ties, this was a happy lifestyle for them. My Father had lost his young wife some years before and his friend was a confirmed bachelor, but my Father did hear he was married sometime later after they went their separate ways. It was about this time, my Father joined a minstrel show performing at various country fairs across America.

It was getting very late, long past the time when us younger ones should have been sound asleep. No one seemed to be making any move in the direction of Bedfordshire, until Mrs. Linstead said, "I think we should thank Mr. O'Neill for entertaining us and give him a rest."

"But he hasn't finished telling us about the minstrel show," one of the girls said.

"And I'm sure he's got lots more 'stuff' to tell us," said Georgie.

"But then," said Mrs. Linstead, "you'd have Mr. O'Neill up all night telling stories and he wouldn't get any rest and neither would you, come now, tomorrow is another day and there might be a surprise tomorrow." We were all wondering what the surprise was going to be.

"Will you tell us now please Mrs. Linstead," Mamie asked.

But she only replied, "You will have to wait and see what tomorrow brings."

It didn't take long for the house to settle down that night. No one was up too early on the morrow and everyone seemed to think it wise to be patient and to wait and see what the surprise would be.

As everyone slept later that next day, we had a very hearty English breakfast. There were eggs, bacon, fat sizzling sausages, fried bread, toast and marmalade, and a big pot of English tea. We youngers were allowed Cambric tea. In case you don't know what that is, it's very weak tea with plenty of sugar and milk. There was milk if we wanted it, but we chose the tea, feeling quite grown up.

Everyone helped clear things away and straighten up the farm-sized kitchen after breakfast. I suppose everyone was thinking; now we will know what the surprise will be.

Soon, gathered in the living room, Mrs. Linstead said, "We are sad that the girls would soon be leaving us," meaning Mamie and I. "Their time here is getting short and soon they will be going back to the convent. We hope that they will come again soon, or better yet, they will be allowed to stay with their Father, and we thought it would be a nice surprise for everyone, and a special memory for the girls to keep, to go to a pantomime. We have tickets for the matinée performance of *Puss and Boots*. So when everyone is ready, we only have a block to walk to the bus stop and the bus stops right outside the theatre."

The Linsteads had attended a pantomime before, but for Mamie and I, this was our first pantomime and we did enjoy it so much. I suppose we were at fever-pitch excitement and I'm afraid that Mamie and I lost our heads during the intermission when we were being treated to ice-cream and we acted rather silly!

The final curtain came down on *Puss and Boots* and there was much animated chatter as people left the theatre, not the least coming from our direction. Thinking back to pantomimes, I have often wondered why the Dame was always played by a man and the principle boy was always a girl!

Instead of going directly home, we were taken into a Lyons Tea Shop for high tea and told we could order anything we liked, what a hard choice to make, especially for little people. Most of our group ordered dishes that came with chips - eggs and chips, fish and chips, sausages and chips, tomatoes on toast and chips, beans on toast and chips. Those dishes were so popular in the Lyons Tea Shops of those days.

Back home at the Linsteads, at the favourite gathering

place in the living room around the fire, and although it had been a fun-filled week, my sister and I were rather sad, for we only had one more day there before we returned to the convent.

When it was getting quite dark outside with the gas lamps on the streets lit, Mrs. Linstead and Irene bustled in with jugs of steaming cocoa, the perfect nightcap for a winter's evening.

We spent the last day with our Father, because it would be a while before we saw him again. He took us to Selfridges - a very large department store in London. Even though it was after Christmas, and Father Christmas wasn't there with his elves, giving treats to children, it was still a magic place to visit. The decorations were still up with many exciting displays throughout the store. Of course, our very favourite place was the toy department, and Daddie soon spotted a table with toys and children's books on sale. He told us each to choose something we would like, Mamie chose a book, I chose a dollie. We seemed to have walked miles that day all over the store and Daddie said, "Do you think you girls are too tired to go for tea here?"

"Oh no Daddie," we cried in unison, "we would love that."

When I look back on that day, I realize how my Father must have scraped and saved to make that special day for us, for he had very little money, and how we took it all for granted! I also look back on the many little surprises he planned for us with his very limited resources and I would like to thank him for all those things, but sadly it is too late, but maybe one day I will be able to tell him.

We were quite tired when we returned home to the Linsteads. It was getting late and there was a friendly moon shining down on us. Everyone was rather subdued as we said our 'goodnights' that last evening.

The last day arrived and Mamie and I were not in a hurry to start, for on this the day we returned to the convent. We all had breakfast together and then got ready for our return to the convent. We had quite a few treasures and souvenirs to pack and many happy memories to take back with us. We said our tearful goodbyes and left with our Father on the journey back to St. Josephs. I think Daddie thought it wise not to say a long goodbye for it would only make the parting more distressful. We were rather subdued, and of course sad, and we didn't really want to share our experiences with the other girls just then. It took us a few days to settle back into the routine of the convent.

I suppose we were luckier than some, even though we had no Mother, we did have a Father, but we didn't see him too often because of circumstances beyond his control. But sadly there were those there who never had any visitors. They may not have had parents or even guardians, for they never talked of parents or guardians, and no one ever came to see the girl who was mentally fragile.

It was impossible not to notice the attention showered upon the girls whose room and board was paid for, or the many gifts and visitors they received. I am ashamed to say us 'poor kids' were quite envious of them. The girls who brushed our contamination from their clothing if we went too close to them were among the 'rich kids'.

The winter seemed very long and very cold that year, and spring seemed to be a long time coming. We made ice slides wherever there was a slope in the asphalt. Sister Mary Audrey, a novice nun, was sliding with us, and she was scolded by the Mother Superior, who frowned upon this fraternization, and sadly it didn't happen again. There was skipping in the playground and playing ball on milder winter days. There were horse chestnut trees, lime trees and plane trees in the playground. It was always exciting to see them show the first signs of spring.

Five years passed. We had been in the convent over six years and it had seemed a very long time. There had been some weekend visits with our Father and sometimes he would be allowed to take us out for the day. During all that time he still tried to get the authorities, the powers that be, to give permission for us to stay with him permanently, and he told us this would probably happen very soon. Mamie was fourteen, and it was assumed she could carry out the homemaking tasks in the absence of a mother, but there still

27

seemed to be a lot of unnecessary red tape to deal with.

Mr. Linstead had been transferred to another town. This meant my Father finding another place to live, which would not be easy. Where could he find accommodation with such a friendly family who took us into their own family and with such a reasonable rent? Sadly, this happy circumstance was never repeated.

My Father's long struggle to get permission from the authorities to keep us with him, and our ordeal at the convent finally ended. It is hard to put into words how we all felt at that time.

Chapter 2

Southend-on-Sea

He looked around in another town, Southend-on-Sea, where he found two rooms with a Mrs. Baker, Ma Baker as we called her. Now there was a character! My Father took us to meet her and to see the rooms on one of the days he was spending with us. I think in our young minds we didn't know quite what to make of her. She gave us tea and biscuits, all along smoking a cigarette. She seemed to be making the most of it with the aid of a pin. No, it wasn't 'funny tobacco', I don't think that was heard of in those days! Mamie often spoke her mind without even thinking and she said, "It's not nice for ladies to smoke cigarettes, and why do you have that pin?" I think Ma Baker was quite surprised to find a convent girl so outspoken and she told Mamie, "You know Mamie, it *don't* do for you to always to say what's on your mind." When we were leaving there, Daddie did tell Mamie she should not have said what she did.

When he asked us what we thought about the rooms. They were really nice bright rooms, the furniture looked comfortable, but 'twas sparse, but we did have some furniture of our own. As you can guess, we were not too long in making up our minds whether we would like to live in Ma Baker's house, it would not be the same as the Linsteads, but it would not be that bad, and, we thought it would be nice to be near the seashore.

With the help of the Linsteads and the aid of a man who had a horse and cart, we were able to move what little furniture and belongings we had. Mamie and I helped as we were older now. No matter how modest a home, it takes a while to find a place for everything and get settled in. I had to be registered at a new school, and Mamie would soon be looking for work. We were very sad when we said our final goodbyes to the Linsteads, for theirs was a true friendship that generated a storehouse of happy memories. They too, would be moving soon to another town quite far, where there was a new job waiting for Mr. Linstead. The Linstead family would be making a new home with new experiences waiting for all of them, happily they all settled in quite well, but like the O'Neills, they missed the old friends and the old neighbourhood. We did keep in touch for some time, but as is often the case in life, we lost contact.

There was only a little gas ring there, no stove. Daddie said Ma Baker told him we might use her stove in the hall, just outside the rooms. She said she didn't do much cooking. Later on, once or twice she cooked a dinner Daddie bought from her for us, but it was only a couple of times, for truly, she was not a very good cook. Daddie paid one shilling and sixpence for our three dinners.

We made much more appetizing things on our own. Daddie sometimes made bacon with fried bread, with tomatoes cooked in bacon fat with salt and pepper, sugar and vinegar, and truly it was delicious. We were always glad when Daddie brought home faggots and pease pudding for supper, another favourite with everyone. There were hot pies, sausage rolls, or Cornish pasties, that came from the bakers, we would have these with chips from the fish and chips shop. I've never known a Londoner turn down jolly old English fish and chips and for our little family it was "A tuppeny and penneth three times please," and for nine pence we had high tea or supper for the three of us! In those days it was always served up in newspaper. I don't think the health rules allow this practice any more.

Other things one could buy at the fish and chips shop were potato fritters, potato slices dipped in batter. You got five large slices for a penny. Also cracklings - a ha'penny worth or a penny worth; bits of batter that fell away from the fish and the fritters that got very crisp bubbling around in the fat - these were put in little grease proof bags. Something else served at fish and chip shops was battered hard roe. I only had it once; it wasn't something I liked too

My "Daddie"
John Aloysius O'Neill

much. Though all of us, Daddie, Mamie and I, quite liked faggots and pease pudding, fish and chips, etcetera, we all had a very strong aversion to tripe, winkles, cockles, whelks, jugged hare, brains and sweetbreads. Some of the foods I call 'very English' behind my mind. And eels, we all thought absolutely repulsive!!

There were many entertainers and buskers along the sea front where they earned their living by just passing around the hat. A favourite show of ours was the Jolly Boys Show. They would often ask people from the audience to come up and do a turn, to recite, sing a song, or dance, and of course, Mamie and I really enjoyed doing our little turn.

Daddie and Mamie and I, were gradually settling in at Ma Baker's. Mamie so far had not done any serious job hunting, but in those days there were untold numbers of magnanimous would-be employers quite willing to take girls just leaving school, no experience necessary, to train them in their homes to be domestic servants. There were domestic service agencies all over England who supplied scullery maids, kitchen maids, parlour maids, chambermaids, cooks general, cooks, butlers, housekeepers, nannies and companions. The girl starting out to be trained on-the-job, might be told that, "Everything is found, even your uniform, and you will have a half day off every other Sunday." She would be up in the morning anywhere between 4:00 and 6:00 a.m., and had to stay until dinner was cleared away in the evening. All this for the princely sum of five shillings per month, probably the equivalent of one American dollar. Employment agencies advertising for domestic servants would have been much more honest and accurate if they had advertised, "Wanted, domestic slaves."

In many situations, as was the case in Mamie's first job, some fourteen year olds were overburdened with the work of cook general and taking care of children also. Affluent people might have quite a few servants, as might titled people, but they kept their purse strings pretty tight when it came to their employees. It was deemed an honour, and you were privileged beyond measure if you worked for Lord and Lady so-and-so. If you have ever watched,

Upstairs, Downstairs, you have the picture. A word in favour of some of these people even though they were quite parsimonious when it came to wages, some did take care of their employees when they could no longer work.

Mamie's first job was with a Mrs. Stevens, whose son lived with her. They ran a small boardinghouse, there were four adults and one child living there besides Mrs. Stevens and her son. Daddie and I went with Mamie for the interview with Mrs. Stevens. She seemed a very nice lady and her son seemed to be affable as well. "Oh yes, we'll take care of her, you've no need to worry about her, she will have a good home with us. She can have a day off every week and some days there won't be too much for her to do. Room, board, uniforms, all found."

It didn't work out that way at all. Every day there was too much to do and it was a struggle to get even one day off every other week. Mamie had all the cleaning to do and it was a large house, most of the meal preparation for eight people and only token help from Mrs. Stevens and her son John. She didn't even have time to eat her meals properly.

The room allotted to her was a mean little place, a narrow hard bed, rickety old washstand, with a chipped jug and basin, wooden chair by the bed, a makeshift closet with rough shelves in it for her clothing. No chest of drawers, lino on the floor, a threadbare scrap of carpet by the bed, and the blankets on the bed were threadbare too. A rough shelf on one wall with an oil lamp on it, also an enamelled candlestick with a half burnt candle. The small dingy window in the room featured an even dingier piece of chintz to serve for the curtain; it matched the limp thing that partially hid the makeshift closet. The only pretense of decoration was an out of date calendar with a picture of poppies on it. To reach this little treasure, you climbed a rickety, uncarpeted staircase to the attic. The bathroom was one long flight of stairs down from there on the next level.

Although we didn't have a lot of furniture, we added a few pictures and ornaments, a quilt, and a mat for the bedside, which made the room quite a bit cheerier. We supplied a small armchair and a little night table with shelves that we found in the market quite reasonably priced, and we replaced the limp chintz that served as draperies.

Mamie did stick it out for some time until her employers started deducting from her pitiful wage for her uniforms, uniforms that were second hand, probably paid for over and over by such deductions and previous exploitation of many teenage girls! And when they rationed the oil for the oil lamp she used and finding fault with her work all the time, Daddie said, "You can't stay there, you'd better just give your notice in."

After she gave her notice in, the remainder of her time there was most unpleasant. They didn't give her any more oil for the oil lamp, she had to use candles, and they refused to give her a reference.

When we moved Mamie's belongings from Mrs. Steven's place, we rented a costermonger's barrow for around a shilling or so. Mrs. Stevens and her son were horrified at the sight of the wheelbarrow. They watched us like hawks as we loaded Mamie's few possessions onto the barrow and Daddie said, "Well Mamie, you're well rid of that place," and Daddie made a special high tea for a little celebration. We had Welsh rarebit, and sausages and tomatoes with salt, pepper, vinegar, sugar, a little bacon fat, a little water, simmered for ten minutes or so. We called it our 'freedom from tyranny tea'. Daddie said Mamie need not look for work right away, but have a little break first.

There were some happy days ahead for us. We never tired of watching the entertainers on the sea front. Sometimes, Daddie would come with us, and for a treat often we had fish and chips for our supper right there on the beach where you could also buy saveloys and pease pudding, or faggots and pease pudding. A saveloy is a very fat wiener and very good with pease pudding - yellow split peas cooked to a mush making a firm pudding-like consistency - and a faggot is very much like a rissole. If you liked shellfish, you could get whelks, cockles, mussels, and winkles, all available on stands along the beach. Some people liked jellied eels and eel pies, but we didn't like those very much, they were not exactly 'our cup of tea'. We did like the pork pies though, and the steak and kidney pies.

There were so many little kiosks and stands along the beach, it seemed you could buy just about anything, and we didn't realize it then, a lot of it was plain junk for the tourist trap, but we thought it terribly exciting. There were deck chairs for hire, photographers would take your picture for a few pennies, fortune tellers and teacup readers. For treats there was cotton candy and peppermint rock inscribed with Southend-on-Sea all the way through. We always wondered at that magic. How did they do it? And there were souvenir shops without number and ice-cream vendors were ever present on the beach.

Every time Mamie and I ventured out on our own, Ma Baker would always admonish us with the same words, "Now you 'gels' be careful, don't you go talking to no strange men, nor no men either, never go in no dark places, always stay where there is lots of light, now you 'ear me well now? You mind what I say now, now be off with 'yer." She really was quite a character, but she did have our welfare at heart. Another one of our haunts was the Kursaal, it had all the attractions of a midway. The main attraction for kids was finding money the merrymakers had dropped. We had a wonderful two weeks or so spent in this happy way, and then Mamie said she would start looking for another job and hopefully it would not be like the last one.

Among the jobs open to girls of fourteen not counting domestic service, were shop girls, waitresses, office juniors, cashiers, and also factory work. Mamie said she didn't think she was suitable for office work and certainly she couldn't be a cashier for she wasn't very good with figures, so that left factory, shop, or waitress work, all foot wearying undertakings.

Quite quickly she got a job in a bright little bakery shop within walking distance of Ma Bakers. There were a few tables, where very light lunches and teas were served. Although the wage was meagre, she did make some tips serving at the tables and working for the owners of the shop was pleasant. If it wasn't too busy in the morning she could have elevenses, her lunch was always provided, and she could have something in the afternoon if she so wished. And happily it was free from the drudge-like quality of her last employment, and when the shop closed at six o'clock she was free to go home, so our little family still had evenings together. Mamie didn't have to wear a uniform; she wore bright smocks that were in keeping with the surroundings. Mamie often brought treats home from the bakery, they would be a day old and she could buy them very reasonably. Sometimes, Mamie would treat Daddie and I to the picture show, and that was always a fun day. We still spent time at the beach and the Kursaal, not as much though, as Mamie was working.

Daddie tried to get Mamie to save a little of her money every month, no matter how small, but Mamie was not the saving kind. Even with Ma Baker's added advice, "Take care of the pennies my 'gel', then the pounds will take care of themselves. You mark my word, my 'gel', cause I never gives 'yer nothing but good advice." I'm sure she meant well, my, but she was nosy, always wanting to know how much Mamie had made in tips that particular day. When I bring to mind Ma Baker, I always see her smoking that stub of a cigarette with a pin and I hear her giving out advice that was 'absolutely gospel' to us 'gels'.

Things seemed to be going along quite smoothly. Daddie was still going around selling things from door-to-door. He would be out on most days only staying home when the weather was too bad. Some days the selling was good, some days it was not so good. Mamie liked her work at the bakery and was doing quite well and I was happy at school, for I've always enjoyed learning.

One day we woke up to quite a commotion in the house. The couple from upstairs were with Ma Baker. We were wondering what all the hustle and bustle was about. We found out later, poor Ma Baker had had a stroke. It was so sad, for to us, she had always seemed so strong and indestructible. Her son and daughter-in-law came to stay with her for a while, as she couldn't manage on her own. Because they had their own home to take care of and they didn't want to be away from it for too long, it was decided that Ma Baker should live with them, and that meant putting the house up for sale. Her son and his wife felt that they could not take care of two places. For us it would mean, again looking for another place to live, something that also had to be faced by the people upstairs. We felt very sad about this for we had become quite attached to Ma Baker in the time we lived in her house. And we all hoped that she would be strong again soon.

Again we made the rounds of vacancies and rooms to rent. We hoped to find something with reasonable rent, not too far distant from Ma Baker's. Ma Baker's son and his wife told us to take our time for no one was standing in line to buy his mother's house.

After a few foot-weary weeks, we did find two fairly large rooms lit by gaslight that were nice and bright, and there was a gas stove that went with them. It was outside in the hall, as many gas stoves seemed to be, but the gas stove was metered. It took pennies and shillings and it would be our responsibility to feed it. This would work out to more than my Father had hoped to pay, for at Ma Baker's and the Linsteads, the gas was included in the rent. Mamie had quite a few meals at the bakery and did bring things from there for the table, so Daddie said we would be able to make ends meet. He said we would use oil lamps and candles sometimes to cut down on the gas. And certainly it would be a far cry from the grim days when the selling was so bad for my Father, Mamie and I had to go to the local mission to ask for bread, and Mamie always made me do the asking. To this day I can remember how ashamed I was at having to do this and it is only in the last year or so that I have been able to talk about it.

Again we rented a wheelbarrow from one of the vendors in the local market because to pay a moving company to move was out of our reach. Mamie's employers gave her a little time off to help with the move. It took a little while as we busied ourselves in making this modest abode into a home, and when we were finished it was quite comfy, cheery and welcoming. We all hoped we would be able to stay put for a while for the upheaval of moving is quite tiring.

It seemed though, this was not to be, for the owners of the shop where Mamie worked, wanted to retire and sell their business. The couple that bought it came with their own ready-made help; they had a son eleven, and a daughter thirteen. They told Mamie they could not afford to keep her on, for their children would be helping in the bakery. Mamie was sad to leave this job for she had enjoyed working in the bakery with such very fair employers. They gave Mamie a very good reference and an extra three months wages. We were wondering what next was in store for our little family.

It seems that we were to be reluctant gypsies, for Mamie got a job in a general store in a little place outside Southend called Rochford. There did not seem to be any vacancies or rooms to rent that were within our means. We did not have a lot of time to look around for the people in the general store needed help quite quickly. There was a gypsy camp in Rochford and my Father heard that they sometimes had a caravan or two to rent. My sister I were full of alarm at the thought that we might have to live there, for in those days, there were rumours, fuelled by ignorance, that gypsies stole babies, put curses on people and what is more, they were terrible thieves.

We found out very quickly that nothing could have been further from the truth and wondered how these fairy stories got started. Members of this community were very friendly to us, all offering help if ever we should need it. For Mr. and Mrs. Lee, who seemed to head the gypsy encampment - I don't know if they would have been called the gypsy king and queen - showed us nothing but kindness. They were an older couple. When I think of Mr. Lee now, he seemed to have an Albert Schweitzer look, and Mrs. Lee was a small woman, her head was covered in grey curls.

They had a grandson, Robert, who hired himself out to harvest crops in Kent where market gardeners allowed people who worked for them to take a little of the good things home to their families. Sometimes Robert would share with us what he brought home. I remember his telling us one time, "I thought I'd bring you a 'foo' peas."

I mustn't forget to mention Mrs. Lee's suet puddings, she made 'spotted dog' or 'spotted dick' as it's sometimes called, jam roly-poly, treacle pudding, jam roly-poly was sometimes called 'dead man's leg'. She made marmalade puddings and ginger puddings and steak and kidney puddings and she never forgot to share with us.

In 1996, during a trip to Ireland, we came across these gypsy caravans and donkeys in Bunratty. The sight of them took me back to my childhood gypsy camp days in England.

The four-wheeled caravan that we rented was a bright yellow with green trim, no pretense of luxury outside or inside. There were two rough-hewn bunks, a table that let down from the wall, and a few stools to sit on. The problem was, what to do with our furniture. Mr. Lee asked us how much furniture we had that would need storing, saying if it was not too much, there was probably room in the large community shed where the group stored items that were not needed presently.

We did not have a lot of furniture, but certainly much more than could be fitted in the caravan. We put our oil heater in the caravan, a couple of oil lamps, a small armchair, replacing the stools that were in there with some padded benches and hassocks. We hung a few pictures on the walls and ornaments on the shelving, made it quite home-like. When more floor space was needed we had to put the chair and the benches on the bunks. We took some of our dishes and pots and pans from our possessions, but there was not room for all of them. The oil stove was our source of heat and our means of cooking and as the top of the stove could only accommodate one cooking utensil at a time we ate a lot of meals cooked in one pot or pan.

Our water came from the community pump, the focal point for socializing where we heard news of the encampment and news of what was going on in the outside world.

The camp used outdoor privies, as there was no such luxury as plumbing anywhere in the encampment.

We had a small galvanized bathtub that was kept outside. For baths we would heat a bucket of water on the oil stove and add about three buckets of cold water to it. Each of us selected a day for a bath, as we couldn't all have one on the same day. On these occasions, we put the chair, benches, etcetera, on the bunks. To ensure privacy when one of us bathed, the other two would stay outside.

Daddie and I were sitting outside one evening beside our little campfire. Mamie was inside having a bath when she called to me. When I went in I saw the problem right away - the oil lamp was flickering and ready to go out.

40

Quickly I lit some candles so she might finish her bath, no home was without candles in those days. Some of us using oil lamps and oil stoves did occasionally forget to check the oil level and were left rather chilly in the dark. It didn't happen too often, as one gets a little wiser as time goes by.

Sometimes there would be large bonfires with anyone joining in who so wished and with each family bringing something for the cookout. Always such delicious meals, saveloys on sticks, with potatoes roasted in the fire. Often there would be a bowl of pease pudding and a tray of faggots and there was no shortage of sweet things, for the women brought a lot of interesting deserts. There was always an enormous pot of coffee bubbling on the fire and gallons of lemonade for the kids.

When everyone had finished eating and most of the clearing up done, out would come a couple of fiddles and a few mouth organs. Our Daddie played the concertina and there would be dancing and singing and spirits were truly and naturally happy without being the bottled kind. So ended the day, and the camp shut down fairly early, as most were early risers. Other times, small groups of people might have their own private campfire just to be together for a quiet time.

Summer was drawing to a close and I had to be registered at the local school. It was a small school and I would be going into grade eight. I really enjoyed learning and schoolwork and would have been quite happy to be a perennial student. That coming year was memorable for me for I had the highest marks in the small school. This would be my last year at school, and then it would be time to join the working world.

I remember my Daddie being very pleased with me. He asked me what kind of work I would like to do. I said I would really like to stay in school, but I knew our finances could not run to this, that I must do my bit to help the family.

Daddie and Mamie and I talked about what kind of work I could do, what job should I seek. I thought I would like to work in an office in the West End of London and this, of course, would mean another move. We never thought living in the gypsy encampment would be a permanent thing and that we would be leaving there sooner or later. The first thing we needed to do though was to find a place to live in London, so when Mamie had her day off, we went up to London to start looking for a place to live.

All The Things I Love
by *Jacqueline O'Neill*

I love to watch the lambs at play,
This bright and sunny day.
I love their little woolly tails,
And the way they frolic thro' the vales.

And how I love the little birds,
It really is beyond all words.
The beauty of these lovely things,
I love their tiny little wings.

I love the trees so fresh and green,
I love a breeze that's not too keen.
For all the warmth, and joy of spring,
I lift my heart to God, and sing.

Chapter 3

And In This Corner ...

Looking for a place to live is not the most pleasant job in the world, and it is very tiring. We had done quite a bit of it in the span of a few years. At that particular time, there seemed to be many vacancies but as our means were very modest our choices were narrowed down considerably. We didn't find anything that first day in London. The only reasonable places were in very rough, run-down neighbourhoods.

We went back to London a couple of days later. Daddie thought when he was going from door-to-door selling that some of the people might know of rooms to rent. I went with him and it seemed to be a very good idea to ask the people if they knew of anything to rent, and we did get some leads this way.

We found a basement suite in a quiet street in Bayswater and the next order of business was to move. We had told the Lee's a few weeks earlier that we would be moving up to London. Robert often took the horse and cart to London and he offered to move our belongings. Our stay with the gypsies had been a pleasant time and more happy memories were woven into the fabric of our lives.

Robert kept his word about the move and helped us move all our possessions. We stopped for fish and chips on the way so we might share a supper with Robert before he returned to Rochford. We packed the tea things and biscuits where we could find them easily to have a cup of tea with our supper. After supper we said a warm farewell to Robert and hoped to see him and his family again, but sadly, our paths never crossed again.

Mamie helped with the move, but she had promised to stay at the general store until they found someone to replace her. It must have been almost a month before they found someone but she left there on very good terms with her employers.

So, it was just Daddie and I getting the new place in order, and as he still had to do his door-to-door selling, a lot of it was left to me.

Mamie was quite sure she could get a job right away and there seemed to be a lot of want ads for juniors in offices. Even though, as I mentioned earlier, Mamie was not the type to save money, she had managed to save a little money so she could help with expenses while looking for a job. Neither of us had to look for too long.

Mamie got a job in a small café in Bayswater that only served light lunches and teas and it closed down at four-thirty. It was very busy and everyone seemed to leave tips. I believe the word tips means *to insure proper service*.

My Daddie took me to my first job interview. It was for a junior clerk at the Shafto Typewriting Agency, run by a Miss Shafto and a Miss Fancourt, both spinster ladies. The offices were in Oxford Street. I got the job and was terribly pleased, but not so pleased when I learned that the wage was only five shillings per week. Filing was among my duties, as was typing envelopes and stuffing them. I set up the print on the Roneo machine and as the junior clerk I usually made the tea for the others in the office. I took the finished work to various offices in the West End, usually on foot, but sometimes I was given bus fare if it was too far. My duties included any of the lesser jobs that nobody else wanted to do.

I did not stay too long at this job, for there was nothing very challenging or interesting about it, in fact it was quite boring. So I started to look over the want ads in the papers. I found an ad for a junior at the British Boxing Board of Control. I didn't want to give up my job before getting another one.

Again, Daddie took me for the interview. The offices for the British Boxing Board of Control at that time were in a very old house on Dean Street. Dean Street being near to or part of Soho, not the most elegant part of London. Many

Here I am, aged fourteen, ready to go to work.

ladies of the evening worked around that area. I am not sure what it is like nowadays, for though I have been back to London many times, I have not been in that particular district. I don't even know if the house is still standing where the Boxing Board of Control had their offices. In fact, I don't even know if there is a British Boxing Board of Control, as such, any more.

Anyway, back to the interview with Mr. Donmall, secretary of the B.B.B. of C. It went quite well. I told him what I did at my other job and that I couldn't start right away for I would have to give notice there first. He said that would be fine, the starting wage is fifteen shillings a week. I thought I hadn't heard right, that was three times as much as I was getting at the typewriting agency. I tried not to sound too excited as I told him what date I would be reporting for work.

Miss Shafto was not too pleased when I told her I had found another job and handed her my notice. I don't think she would have found it too easy to fill the job for five shillings a week. I was quite anxious to start my new job, and some of the duties I had were similar to those in my last job.

The first order of business on my arrival was to meet the rest of the staff. There was Miss Cross, who was Mr. Donmall's secretary; Mr. Street was the overseer in our office, Dickie Moore, another clerk, Dave Brandon, Doris Faulkner, Winnie Whitmore, Billy Williams and myself. I was the youngest in the office, the other girls were around sixteen. I think Miss Cross may have been in her forties, and Dickie was in his twenties, with Dave Brandon about eighteen or so, Mr. Street probably in his fifties. The two inspectors attached to the Board, Mr. Carl and Jimmie Lambert came in for meetings quite often.

The offices were in quite an old house, the ceilings were quite high, and the windows were always grimy. The big boardroom had a solid mahogany table, leather chairs, and pictures of the old time boxers around the walls. Fighters like John L. Sullivan, Gentleman Jim Corbett, Jack Dempsey, Bob Fitzsimmons, Jack Johnson, are just some that

I can call to mind that were around the walls in that boardroom. We had a little staff room in the back, where the big scale was on which the boxers were weighed. There always seemed to be a few pairs of boxing gloves in our staff room.

Again I did filing, typed envelopes and stuffed envelopes, I set the type on the Roneo machine, but the other girls shared the tea making duties. There were big leather-bound ledgers where copies of letters, minutes of meetings, licenses, and other documents were filed. It was my job to make the copies and file them in the correct ledgers. I'm quite sure this method of copying has not been used for many a long year, for it used damp rags, sheets of cardboard, then the ledger was put into a heavy press.

The work at the British Boxing Board of Control was interesting. We met many of the boxers of that time and all of us girls collected autographs. Boxers seemed to have one thing in common, they were all quite shy. We met Joe Louis and Tommy Farr; Tommy had to come back for his hat on one occasion and blushed before all of us girls. Others were Walter Nuesel from Germany; Max Baer the madcap American boxer, Benny Caplan, Norman Snow, Jack Doyle, and Larry Gains. Jack Peterson was a very gentlemanly boxer from Wales who retired from the ring because his sight was going. There were also some very sad ex-fighters that the Boxing Board Benevolent Fund helped, they made your heart ache. There were occasions when Mr. Donmall gave us all tickets to the championship fights, giving each of us girls a box of chocolates. I don't know if the men got anything.

I remember Daddie always liked boxing matches, so we went together on these occasions. He had seen John L. Sullivan fight and Gentleman Jim Corbett and quite a few of the others. I don't think I ever liked boxing and I sure don't like it now. I didn't like violence, but I did enjoy the work there. It was interesting meeting the boxers, the seconds, the managers, and all the other sports people that went with the boxing world. Mr. Street was a bit serious, and Mr. Carl was distant, but Jimmie Lambert was a little, round, jolly, man.

I wonder where the pictures of the old time boxers that were in the boardroom are today. I wonder if they would have been kept or discarded. The active boxers I met when I worked at the Boxing Board of Control would be the old time boxers now, and I imagine their pictures would decorate the walls of the present-day Boxing Commissions. I don't think any of them would still be around and maybe their 'brief moment of glory' is too long ago for anyone to remember.

There was an electric heater in our staff room and we office girls used to turn it onto its back to make our soup from E.D. Smiths', oxtail and tomato soup cubes, we just added water. The heater worked quite well, but I don't think it was terribly safe.

It seemed the girls exclusively used the staff room; the men ate their lunches at their desks. Miss Cross was not too friendly and didn't really like us asking for autographs, but she couldn't do much about it. She bossed us around even though we were not under her supervision, just Mr. Street's. Sometimes she would make us work a half day on Saturday, and on these occasions she sent someone, usually me, to buy some large fruit buns that came with butter from Lyons Tea Shops and something fishy for her own lunch from the delicatessen. We were not paid for going in on Saturdays, but happily it didn't happen too often. I guess this is why they provided something for us to eat.

Mamie came back from Rochford, they had found someone to replace her in the general store, and now it was her turn to look for a job in London. Without too much looking she found a job in Cadby Hall where they made and packaged all the Lyons products for the market and for all the Lyons Tea Shops.

Wherever we were living, Mamie and I would check the local community hall to see what activities were offered. Most of the halls had dance and drama groups, and these always appealed to us and we did learn quite a bit from these little groups. There was a small dance studio in Maida Vale. It was very reasonable. I went there for a few sessions. The owner of the school asked me if I would like to help teach the younger children ballet and tap dancing. I was quite delighted at this prospect, for she said, then there would be no charge for my lessons.

I had learned quite a bit at the British Boxing Board of Control, but thought it was time for a change. Daddie was getting quite weary of selling from door-to-door and didn't go out as much or stay out as long, so I thought if I got a waitress job where there were tips, I could help quite a bit that way.

I took a job in a restaurant in the West End. It was very busy and I was very tired at the end of the day, but I did make quite a bit there, but it seemed that cocktail waitresses did a lot better than restaurant waitresses, so I quickly changed. This work was quite a bit more pleasant than the restaurant work and people were not as rushed and I met many interesting people.

There were other restaurant jobs along the way and I also worked for friends in a pub in the Kensington district, although I was underage for that job. No one caused any problems about it. I worked there from about four until nine. We had a half hour for supper break around six or six-thirty. To this day, I can hear the Cockney bartender telling me on one of these breaks, 'Ave a bloomin' good blowout mate."

"What," I said, "on cheese and pickles?" for that seemed to be the fare that particular evening. I can see that chap's happy grin, but his name escapes me.

I quite liked that little job at the pub, there were so many friendly people coming in there. I can't remember there being any ugly drunks. As with the people in the cocktail lounge, the customers there were more relaxed, not so much in a hurry as customers in restaurants.

In my quest to keep money coming in I was a companion to an elderly lady at one point. I wrote letters for her, took her to the hairdressers and shopping. We went everywhere by taxi, and shopping, of course, was delivered.

I took care of a little boy for a while, both the parents worked, and I had a stab at that cook general business, which turned out to be strictly 'slave labour'.

49

Then there was my job at the Home and Colonial; I was a cashier there in the fish and poultry 'cage'. There were four of us girls in the one cage and quite a few cashiers in the store as a whole. I was happy that my cash always balanced and I never had to make up any deficiencies. The store where I worked was in Edgeware Road. I was sent to a small Home and Colonial in Putney for a while as a relief cashier, quite a different pace from the hustle and bustle of Edgeware Road. I went back again to the big store after a while and they wanted me to work in the office there, but I said I preferred working with the public, so I stayed where I was.

Becoming A Man
by *Janine Allison Dahm*

Where are you going, oh child so young?
Why do you leave all your toys and fun?
This war is for men, strong, big and brave,
Men who battle and fight, for their country, to save.
Alas, you must join them, the boy that you are,
To save your own country and keep Her from harm,
Where are you going, oh child so young?
Your going to war, a man you'll become.

Chapter 4

London at War

In September 1939, England declared war on Germany after Adolph Hitler sent his Panzer divisions storming through and quickly defeating Czechoslovakia and Poland. What a place London was in wartime with people crowding in from all over the world. It must have been the most vibrant place on earth at that time and despite the sadness and tragedy of war, there was an urgency that could only be found in London. No one knew what tomorrow might bring, so I think the general feeling was, we have today - live it to the fullest.

We met many boys in the military services from other countries as well as our own, all lonely for their homes and families. Sometimes my Daddie would bring service people home and we'd share a meal with them and they liked to receive a friendly letter from us now and again.

There was nothing elaborate or fancy about the meals because many things were rationed. Meat was rationed, but one could get liver and kidneys and heart, and sausages, but there was quite a bit of filler in sausages. I think we got one egg per week. Tea and sugar and butter and margarine were rationed also, but we could get dried eggs, and you could make a fairly nice omelette with these. Bacon was rationed too; I think we might have got two ounces of bacon per week. We could always get potatoes, but not always onions, and fresh fruit was quite scarce also, and we could get fish, not very much cheese.

We usually managed to come up with something. I remember a lot of the restaurants in wartime used to serve jugged hare, boiled cod and parsley sauce, sweetbreads, brains and the unforgettable Spam, and there were a lot of pigeons eaten through the wartime, but with all the moaning

Mummie Orsi much later, in 1964 at Brighton Beach. Mummie is on the left, her mother on the far right. Her sister and nephew in between.

and groaning and grumbling that some people did about rationing, there always seemed to be something to eat.

I remember quite well two American boys Daddie brought home one time, they had dinner with us, one was named Clarence and the other was Joel. Clarence came from Rhode Island and Joel was from Maine. It gave one a good feeling to bring a little brightness to these lonely boys in a strange country. We wrote to them for quite a while and then their letters stopped. We were informed that they were missing in action, and were greatly saddened by that. We prayed that they would be found and that they would be safe.

I remember an occasion talking to some prisoners of war, how sad they seemed, how vulnerable, not monsters, just boys who had to do what they were told to do, just like our own boys, the Allies. They didn't want to fight, they didn't want war any more than we did.

An Italian friend of mine, whom I called Mummie Orsi, because she was very motherly to me, had to manage her restaurant without the aid of her husband. He was put into an internment camp because he had been born in Italy. He died in that camp of pneumonia, a very sad and broken man. He wasn't even forty, and Mummie Orsi was left to bring up two boys on her own.

The IRA was sympathetic to the German cause and many people of Irish lineage were questioned by the authorities, as I was myself, on more than one occasion.

It was said that the British spirit was indomitable through those trying wartime years and a sense of humour helped a lot at that time. There was a cartoon character Mr. Chad and his, "Wot, no beer? Wot, no cigs?" comments, whose nose and fingertips hung over the wall, was used a lot to inform us that there was none of this, or none of that. Then there was Billy Brown of London Town, the cartoon character used in posters in the Underground who told you not to tear back the netting on the windows and that it was placed there so the glass wouldn't shatter in the bombing. It showed a passenger tearing back the netting on the subway train windows and Billy Brown telling him, "I trust you'll

I trust you'll pardon my correction, that stuff is there for your protection.

Wot, no Guinness?

pardon my correction, that stuff is there for your protection."

Someone else wrote underneath, "I trust you'll pardon my intrusion, that stuff is there for your confusion." Another one said, underneath the original, "Thank you for the information, but we can't see the bloody station!" There was a 'diamond' shaped space left 'unnetted' in the middle of the window so that you could look through to check the name of the station.

The subway trains were so packed in those years, with so many more people in London at that time. In addition to all the service people from many countries, there were a lot of war correspondents, and a lot more various countries' embassy people. I met and chatted with two very well known and interesting war correspondents at a restaurant in Fleet Street called the *Falstaff*. Several embassy workers and many service people came to Mummie Orsi's restaurant and we got to know them, as well as one could in those times.

I recall writing to a friend from Yugoslavia for quite some time, then suddenly the letters stopped, sometimes it was best not to know why. A Polish friend wanted to learn more English. He asked me if I would teach him and I told him he would be better off with a friend of mine who taught elocution and French, and as he spoke French, it would be a lot easier for him. She had taught me the basics of French, most of which, I've all but forgotten now. She also taught piano and I picked up a few useful hints from her.

There was no shortage of companions to see a show with, have dinner, lunch or tea, or maybe go dancing with, nothing serious, just good friends. As I look back on those days, it makes me sad and very ashamed that I left my father home alone so much. I could and should have, spent more time with him. I fear I must have been very selfish in those days, a period of time in my life when I thought I was the most important person in the world!

Mamie by this time had moved out of our little home, leaving just Daddie and I. Mamie was working in a munitions factory. I still did some part time work in the catering business as the money was quite good, so Daddie didn't have to go door-to-door so much as before.

We saw quite a bit of Mamie who had moved into what we called a bedsitter. It was a very pleasant room and her landlady and landlord seemed quite nice people. She had made friends with some of the people she worked with, as I had too. Sometimes I would invite them for tea so Daddie could meet them.

There were two sisters from Gibraltar, refugees who came to London with their family. Maria and Conseula came to tea a few times and met Daddie and they took me to meet their family. In fact their mother put my first pair of pierced earrings in place, sitting on a kitchen chair by a very large window. Mama put a darning needle into a flame on a gas stove, pierced my ears with it, dabbed them with peroxide, and put the earrings in. I think I prefer the present day method, not quite so primitive. Many girls and women from Gibraltar had pierced ears.

I took Maria and her sister, Consuela, to one of the senior's homes when our little dance group entertained there, a new experience for them. We liked going to the care homes and the group homes, it seemed to bring a bright spot to their day.

On occasion Daddie and I would enjoy a game of draughts, or checkers as we call it here. He loved to read, especially liking westerns and he loved to play his concertina. He did so enjoy making meals for me, but he wasn't the greatest cook! Another of his favourite things was when we would go to a show together. I often wonder what he would think of the world today if he were to see it now? To say that he would be astounded is an understatement indeed, and certainly he would be saddened and shocked by these latest acts of terrorism and bio-terrorism that our world is dealing with today.

I don't know if I would be correct in saying that as a Londoner we got used to the Blitz, the bombings, the sirens, the blackouts, but we certainly learned to live with it, we had to, for there was nothing we could do about it. I felt so sad for the people who used to go down to the Underground

The Dancing Years.

to sleep. They had to put up with so much, no privacy at all and no quiet 'til the trains stopped running. Sometimes drunk people getting off the trains fell into them while they were trying to sleep.

On the streets there were sandbags everywhere. There were water reservoirs and signs to tell you where the nearest ARP (Air-Raid Precautions) station was, signs directing you to the nearest hospitals. There were above ground air-raid shelters built of brick and concrete blocks right outside where Daddie and I were living. There were benches inside them, but we failed to see the wisdom of these, for we never did see them used by anybody.

The Blitz mostly at night, was however, ever-present, it never let you rest. Worrying about the next air-raid was often worse than the attack itself. Behind my mind I can sometimes still hear the intermittent wail of the warning sirens and the anxiety that they caused. The steady all-clear signal did bring relief, but with it came concern for those friends or neighbours who may have been injured or even lying dead amongst the shrapnel and debris filling the streets.

Where we lived in the basement flat on Denbigh Terrace we had an elderly upstairs neighbour, Josephine Ratsell. When the air-raid warning siren sounded she would rush down to the basement, and into the coal cellar, which was part of our place. She would be terrified and literally shaking like a leaf.

The only thing that calmed Josephine at all was when I would join her in that tiny coal cellar, put my arms around her and talk to her. I would tell her to think of lovely English gardens and pretty flowers and sunny summer days.

Something new were Belisha beacons, designed by Sir Leslie Hore-Belisha, a black and white metal post with an orange glass ball on top. They designated pedestrian crossings, where there were two rows of large steel studs, the rows being about six feet apart, maybe more, and the studs being about one foot apart, going to the other side of the street. The vandals who were never happy unless destroying things, lost no time in breaking the glass balls on top of the posts, and soon all the glass balls were replaced with metal ones.

One morning, just after the all-clear signal, I went outside to see what was left of the world. As I stepped onto the street I glanced up to the sky and saw something bright and silvery floating down. It landed almost at my feet. I carefully picked it up, and discovered that it was a piece of shiny fabric made of material unfamiliar to me. I remember thinking to myself that there was enough of it to make a very pretty Juliet cap. It wasn't until several days later that I was able to find out that the material was a small piece of what was left of a Barrage Balloon; obviously shattered somehow during the raid.

I shall never forget those marvellous uplifting wartime songs, among them; *I'll Be Seeing You, Lili Marlene, I'll Get By, The Last Time I Saw Paris, White Cliffs of Dover, Bluebird on My Windowsill, I'll Never Smile Again,* all the songs and singers of that era bring back so many memories, so much nostalgia. I think my very favourites of that time were, *I'll Be Seeing You* and *Lili Marlene*.

On December 7, 1941, almost the end of the year and everyone was shocked beyond belief when the United States naval fleet at Pearl Harbour was bombed, a tragedy that brought the United States into the war.

At times it seemed hard to remember the days of peacetime when there was no rationing, hearts were lighter, faces were brighter, and people were not compelled to carry around those little cardboard boxes containing gas masks. In spite of all the hell, most of the theatres in the West End still carried on, put on their shows. After theatre suppers, dancing and many, many girls falling in and out of love with a new heart-throb every other week.

In the Blitz, there were lots of funny little things that took place, minor inconveniences. For example one of my fellow cocktail waitresses, Nancy Wilkins showed up for work in a terribly wrinkled waitress uniform one day. Bomb explosion vibrations had knocked out the electric bulbs in her residence, although the power had still been on, a

Modelling days so long, long ago.

blackout within the blackout, she had ironed her uniform in the dark!

Almost the end of 1942 another year gone. We had been at war for over three years. In the beginning people said, "This won't last long, we'll soon put Jerry in his place." It didn't happen though. There still didn't seem to be an end in sight.

It was about this time that I got a job modelling in an art school. They wanted a girl who was fair, someone who would look good with pastel colours and they chose me, and I was glad they did. I was also doing work for two other artists. I was able to leave the catering business and I did find the work more pleasant, but sometimes got a bit stiff from sitting still or standing still for so long. There was always someone there to spoil me and bring me tea or coffee, etcetera. And working for the private artists, their wives would always bring me a nice tea tray and I found this a lot better than waiting on someone else!

Daddie didn't go from door-to-door much any more; there wasn't the need for it as there was before we two sisters began to earn. I think it must have been hard for him to fill his days when I was gone all day long. He liked to go to the local park and feed the birds and was always glad when we had a visitor or Mamie would bring her friends to the house.

There was a form of entertainment that was quite popular during the war years; in fact it may have been born in that era, the News Theatres. They would bring you up to date on all the news at home and abroad, and there would always be what they called a short, and a couple of cartoons. It was a good way to fill an hour or so, when one had time to spare.

The instructor of the dance group I was with liked to enter her girls in the British Ballet organization exams. I was quite pleased to come away with honours in this exam and I quite enjoyed helping the little kids with their ballet and tap. All in all I kept pretty busy, and never gave a thought about getting serious with any boyfriend.

I bought myself a bike and enjoyed riding all over

London. The drivers of those big, red, London busses weren't too happy with the bicycle riders dodging in and out of traffic.

One particular bike trip I took with my friend, Truda. I had met Truda's parents briefly. Her father was from Czechoslovakia and her mother from the Midlands. Her father had an old world charm and her mother was a very comfortable woman. It was a lovely summer's day. Truda and I took a picnic lunch to Hockley Woods, an area not too far from London, and we gathered bluebells there. We filled our baskets with them and the fragrance was delightful.

At that time theatres were showing a lot French films with English sub-titles and Truda and I saw quite a few of them. It seemed quite the fashionable thing to do. I remember what a weepy thing *Mayerling* was with Charles Boyer, who was quite the heart-throb of that era, and Danielle Darrieaux.

I bought a little radio, it would be nice for Daddie. He could listen to the news and the shows *Music While You Work, Jack Warner, Litel Gel, Arthur Askey, Nausea Bagwash, Tommy Trinder* and *Sandy Powell*, making the day a little cheerier for him.

We were not by any stretch of the imagination, affluent, but we had come quite a way since those sad days of convents and family separations of the not too long ago.

1944 - We had been at war over four years. How weary all of the fighting forces must have been of the horror and terror of war. So many made the supreme sacrifice, so many maimed - their lives never to be the same! The whole world was war weary. All because a monster named Adolph Hitler was still filled with hatred and hungry for power.

Even in the midst of war, springtime brought a promise of better things to come, flowers bloomed, trees put on their new dresses and birds still sang as they built their nests, and children continued to laugh and play.

I had never been much for parties; quite frankly, I found them quite tedious, shallow, and a waste of time. I liked people, but I am certainly not much of a drinker.

When a friend asked me if I would like to go to a little gathering she was having, I said I didn't think so. She said "you might like it, it could be fun," so reluctantly I agreed to go.

There were two other couples there besides my friend and her companion. There was also one chap without a companion, they were all in the Canadian Air Force. After introductions all round I soon realized that I was needed for a fill-in and I was not too happy about it, but made the best of it and tried to be gracious to this lonely chap. As we talked it became apparent that we had many of the same thoughts, and many of the same ideas. He seemed to be such a gentle soul and was missing his home in Quebec so much. I noticed too, that he wasn't much of a drinker either. There was an old wind-up phonograph and we danced a little, sang a few songs around the piano, got to know a little of the other people there and had a bite to eat. All in all, it was not too bad an evening and I was rather glad that I went.

Tony, for that was my companion's name asked if he might see me home. On the way in the taxi he said he would like to see me again, and I thought I would like to see him again. He said he would phone me on his next leave. We didn't have a private telephone, but there was a phone in the hall for the use of the tenants in the house, not the best arrangement, but certainly better than no phone at all. As I was drifting off to sleep, I went over the events of the evening and was quite happy with them.

Over the next little while I found myself thinking about this lonely chap from Canada. About two weeks later when I came home from work, there was a message on the hall table saying that Tony had phoned and he would phone again later.

I just had time to bathe when I was called to the phone, it was Tony saying he was on three days leave and he would like to see as much of me as he could. I told him I would like to spend the evening with my Father and it was getting rather late, but arranged to see him the next day for dinner. He said he would call for me in a taxi.

When he came the next day I did not invite him in, and only recently have I been able to think or talk about the reasons why, and some of these things I'd rather not remember. Frankly, I was ashamed of our humble home, of being poor, and that my Father didn't have a very important job. When I look back, I feel bad and very sad at having had these feelings. I never did invite Tony in to meet Daddie, thinking he would think less of me if he knew our circumstances.

Tony and I got to know a little more of each other in our next meeting. He told me he was an intelligence officer, and had four sisters and one brother. The brother was doing missionary work in Africa. One of his sisters was married, two were in a religious life, and one was home with his parents. We talked of hobbies and things we liked to do, books we'd read, and things like that. We found we had so many likes and dislikes in common. He hoped we might go to a show the next day. I told him it might be hard to get tickets unless you booked ahead. He said he'd do what he could. When we said goodnight, I realized to my dismay I liked this person more than I wanted. Of the service people I had known, he seemed somehow different and I was thinking about him too much! Again I told myself, it is not the time to get serious about anyone and certainly a commitment to another person was not in the plans for my life. Somehow I got the feeling that Tony had these serious thoughts also, but there was something else I couldn't quite understand.

The next day at work so many thoughts were tumbling around behind my mind. When he phoned he said he had tickets for *See How They Run*, a comedy that had been running for a long time in London. He wanted us to go for a bite to eat first. I told him I wanted to eat dinner with my Daddie.

The show was light and quite amusing. It didn't take too much concentration to follow it. During intermission, he said he was sad that this would be the last time we would be together 'til his next leave, and I was feeling rather sad also. "I know we haven't known one another very long, but I think I'm falling in love with you," he told me, and maybe I was feeling the same way too. "I wish we could be together always," he said. I told him, wartime was not the best time to make plans, certainly not lifetime plans. "No," he said, "it's more than that." I thought that he must be married, and I said as much, and when he replied in the negative, I thought that he must be engaged, for he was quite a few years older than I. "No, I am not engaged either, I am a priest, and feel that I have not been fair with you, maybe I should have told you this at our first meeting."

"Hardly," I said, "that's not something one would talk about when meeting a person for the first time, not knowing if they would ever see that person again."

We then both decided that maybe it would be better if we did not see one another again. I suppose I was more than a little shocked, for up until that time in my life, I hadn't known that priests went out on dates and didn't think that it was a usual thing for them to do, and having the convent in my background, always thought the religious were somewhat above humans.

(I realize now at this late stage in my life, that they certainly are human, they too have their faults and weaknesses, and certainly no one wears a halo. I'm pretty sure though, even today, when the discipline isn't nearly as stringent as it was back then, that it is not usual for priests to go out on dates. Such encounters can be put down to the loneliness and heartbreak of war.

There are probably more than a few in the Catholic church that hope one day there may be a change in the laws of the church whereby priests might marry, also nuns, as most other denominations are able to do).

It had been a few weeks since Tony and I decided it would be better if we didn't see one another gain. He phoned early one evening in the fall hoping we could have dinner together. I shouldn't have, but I agreed, for I was almost getting resigned to not having him in my life any more. I looked forward to seeing him with a gladness, but also a sadness, for I knew the heartache would start all over again.

We went to our favourite restaurant. We knew the staff there quite well and they were very attentive. They seemed to know how people felt about one another looking on them benignly and beaming all over. Tony and I agreed that we had missed one another terribly and we were so happy to be together again. We seemed to be made for one another, just made to be together.

The Loveliest Things There Are
by *Jacqueline O'Neill*

God made the Earth, He made the Sun,
He made the flowers, every one.
He made the lambs, and birds so small,
He made us creatures, all, and all.

He thought awhile when making me,
He thought to fill my heart with glee.
He sent you to me one fine day,
That lovely sunny day in May.

Of all the lovely things there are,
Yes, even the very loveliest star,
There's nothing to compare to you,
I pray that you'll be ever true.

Tony said he had something very important to tell me. He said he had thought long and hard about us being together. That God had made us for one another and it just had to be that he would leave the church and we would be married. That is what we both wanted. A warning light went on in my head. No it can't be. He was a priest first and if things didn't work out for us and if he became disenchanted, he might hate me and long for the life he had before.

All that aside, he was a chaplain in the Air Force. It was wartime, he couldn't leave just like that. You couldn't have someone you loved disgraced and under a cloud. No, we must put aside personal feelings, and do the honourable thing. But we did agree to keep seeing one another as long as he was in England hoping it wouldn't prove too hurtful.

As time went on, we were getting to know more about each other. I learned that his father was in a seminary for a while as a young man. He had not taken any vows when he met and fell in love with his mother. He left the seminary and a while later they were married. His father had studied law before entering the seminary, and joined a law firm after leaving the seminary. He later became a Supreme Court Judge. The partner in the law firm, who was his godfather, later attained a very high official position in Canada. The Lord surely does move in mysterious ways for instead of just one religious to do His work, there were four.

I told him of my mother leaving when I was very young. Something he said, that he couldn't understand. "My mother would have loved you," he said. I thought that was one of the nicest things he could have told me, it made me feel very warm inside. He said it saddened him that I had grown up without a mother for his mother was very important to him. He said he loved her dearly. I told him I had a sister who was born a twin, but her little brother had died at birth. I told him of our time in the convent, a time I would rather not remember.

Tony and I spent every minute we could together, we knew this wasn't the wisest thing to do for it would make it so much harder when we came to say goodbye. Once again he mentioned leaving his vocation. I said it wouldn't be the right thing to do. Half-heartedly he agreed.

1945 - I had moved into a room of my own a short time previously and Mamie had moved back in with Daddie. I had been so preoccupied with my own life, that I hadn't spent a lot of time with my Father and I did feel badly about that.

One day I popped around to see him and there was a Canadian army chap there. He was looking for Mamie's friend, Nan, because she often came to visit. I visited with my Daddie for a while, and as I was leaving, Allan, for that was his name, asked if he might see me home. I said that would be all right. At my door, he had bent to kiss me goodnight but I quickly told him that I didn't kiss boys that I didn't know. I just shook his hand. He wanted to see me on his next leave. I said I would think about it, then dismissed it from my mind.

I saw Tony whenever he came to London.

One afternoon I went to see my Daddie and who should be there, but Allan. He wasn't looking for Nan this time, he was looking for me. He had a couple of days leave and would like to spend some of it with me if I agreed. Maybe we could go out for dinner together?

Where I lived, there were a couple of very nice restaurants in the area. One of them was called the *Green Parrot*. There was also a rather nice tea shop called the *Majestic* which we settled on. I remember the windows of the *Majestic*, crinolined ladies in pastel hues decorated all the windows. It was a cheery place, warm and comforting. They made the tastiest corned beef sandwiches. There was cucumber, tomatoes, lettuce and beets, or beetroot as we used to call it, and of course, mayonnaise. They must have been very good, because I do remember them to this day.

While we ate, Allan told me he was from Calgary, Alberta. He lived with his parents before joining the army. He had a brother who was still in school. He had a sister who was killed in 1944. I had no idea where Calgary, Alberta was, and I suppose I wasn't that much interested at the time.

I think he may have been shocked that Nan was married and had a six year old son. And I said, "It's wartime, things happen, people get lonely." I thought she may have been lonely too.

He told me a little of his life in Canada. His extended family was quite large; there were two grandma's and a grandpa, numerous aunts, uncles, and cousins. He was probably missing all of this in England.

I wondered how his sister had been killed and asked. He told me that she had been married to a pilot in the Canadian Air Force. They were riding on a motorcycle, she was on the pillion seat, and they were travelling in Eastern Canada, when the motorcycle hit a tree. They hadn't been married very long, she was only twenty-four. Not too long after this, her husband was killed flying over France.

After dinner I suggested that we should go back and have a little visit with Daddie before we left him for the evening. "But before we go," he said, "can I see you again on my next leave?"

Allan, the day he joined the Canadian Army.
He was just seventeen years old.

"Well," I replied, "I don't want to make any commitments."

He added that he still had another days leave, but I said I had other things to do and that maybe I would see him on his next leave. Daddie said he quite liked him, "He seemed a nice chap."

Mamie had met him and she quite liked him. I can't say that I found myself thinking about him all the time, the way I did with Tony, even though Tony was a lost cause.

Maybe some girls think about 'knights in shining armour', and 'happily ever after' plans, in their very early teens, but I was never one of those girls. I liked things they way they were. I enjoyed being with my friends, activities with the dance and drama groups. I liked reading, sketching, going for walks and observing nature. I liked swimming and biking, but all this had changed since I had met Tony.

Our time spent together seemed to be an exercise in futility, knowing we were only prolonging the final parting, but events beyond our control decided for us. Tony was ordered back to Canada. Our final goodbyes were sad indeed and I felt desolate at the thought of never seeing him again.

Allan's sister, Edna May, killed in a motorcycle accident, and her husband Maurice McLear, later killed while flying for the RCAF.

Chapter 5

War Bride

English War Bride
by Janine Allison Dahm

Where are you going, little girl so lovely?
Across the big ocean, to live in a new country.
Say goodbye to English teas, and chubby English robins,
Tuppences, and ha'pennies, butter tarts
And Bacon Bonces.

Where are you going, Oh little girl so fair?
To Canada, Oh Canada,
To live with my soldier there.

I hadn't heard from Allan for some time, I wondered if he had been sent back to Canada. One day he phoned and said he had been in sick bay with tonsillitis. He was coming up on leave in a couple of days, could he meet me then. I said okay, why not. I thought it would be a distraction.

We went to the *Green Parrot*. There wasn't much to choose from on their menu that evening. I do remember they had jugged hare, boiled cod and parsley sauce and sweetbreads, all equally revolting. I think we must have settled for braised Spam, and for dessert, a good old wartime standby that went by the illustrious name of cabinet or diplomat pudding. We never knew what went into this diplomat pudding, and we were diplomatic enough, not to ask.

Even though the fare was plain indeed, we spent a pleasant hour or so in the *Green Parrot*. We talked of likes and dislikes, favourite things and unfavourite things. Allan told me he was seventeen when he joined the army. He didn't even shave at that time. His first choice had been the air force, but his eyesight was not good enough. The military wanted to send him to officer training, but he wanted to enlist as a private. In no time at all he became a staff sergeant, but he still didn't want to be an officer.

I soon found out that Allan was a strong-willed and determined person. One evening he stayed with me well past the time that London transportation systems had shut down. He was to tell me later that on his way walking back to his quarters, going through Hyde Park, a stranger had accosted him.

"Got the time Canada?" asked the stranger pointing to Allan's watch.

Allan had been warned of this trick often used by would-be muggers, intent on theft or worse. In a split second Allan landed a round house right on the man's chin, laying him out cold on the grassy floor of Hyde Park. Allan had then made a rapid departure.

Allan often said he would like to have a little visit with my Father. I knew Daddie would enjoy that. I felt no embarrassment about entertaining him in these modest surroundings, as I would have done entertaining Tony there, even though I knew there was no snobbishness in Tony and no false pride. His humility was one of the qualities that attracted me to him. I found him to be a totally unselfish person. Allan and I had a happy evening with Daddie and he was glad of our company.

Eighth of May 1945, V-E Day - The war in Europe was over. There was dancing in the streets. There was great rejoicing, and great sadness for all the boys who wouldn't be coming back, for all the mindless destruction and the horrendous upheaval of lives that war brought in its wake.

I knew that Allan cared about me, and I quite liked him, not in the same way that I loved Tony. However, I was indeed surprised when Allan asked me to marry him. He knew my feelings but still thought we would fit well together. How to answer, to make the right decision.

Would things go well for us or would this deep friendship with Tony, that was more than friendship, stand in the way forevermore.

"I must have a little time to think about it," I told him.

"I hope not too long," he said, "for I don't know what's happening with the army."

If I said yes, would I be fair to Allan, or to myself? I had told Allan that I cared about him, but not in the same way as I cared about Tony. Would these feelings be enough, would they last to survive all the ups and downs, good times and the bad times that come with every life. At the same time I knew there was no future in a life with Tony.

I phoned Allan a couple of nights after this and told him to take care of all the military red tape and to tell me what kind of civilian red tape I must attend to.

He said, "You mean you're really saying yes."

"I wouldn't do all of that if I weren't, now would I, and it is nice that we're both Catholics isn't it?"

War Brides Service
by *Janine Allison Dahm*

Although your soldier's gone away,
A proud war bride, must you always stay.
You've done your service, to your country too,
You loved a soldier; and saw him through.

In the days of war and constant fight,
Your love was a comfort to him each night.
When his courage, was about to fall,
Your love helped him stand strong, brave and tall.

And in the darkness of the black of space,
Your soldier boy, would imagine your face.
Your delicate beauty and love-filled eyes,
Would muffle the bomber planes in the skies.
Your love brought him through the battlefields,

Of grenades, and guns, and pistols wield.
When the battle ended,
You journeyed into life,
As a little English war bride,
To be this soldier's wife.

But now the heavenly bugle,
Has called your soldier home.
No more wars or battlefields,
Will your soldier roam.

And you are left all alone,
With many tears now dried.
Remember as a war bride,
Your country is your pride.

July 27, 1946. On the steps of the Harrow Road Registry Office in Paddington. (left to right) Marie Harrington, Babs Smythe, Allan, me, little June Harrington, Nella and her sailor brother, whose name now escapes my memory.

It took a few weeks to get everything in order and we were married in Paddington registry office in Harrow Road, on the morning of the 27th of July in 1946. (The Catholic Church never considered civil marriages valid). A very quiet ceremony, no fuss and no reception, as many weddings were at that time of war. It was a Saturday, and Allan was due back in barracks by Monday. I now feel the pangs of guilt, for I hadn't wanted my Father at the ceremony. I felt it would have reminded me too much of the poverty I was trying to get away from and put behind me. My Father had been married when he was very young in the United States and his wife had died soon after their marriage. His second marriage to my mother had taken place later in life and when she left us, I realize now, how very lonely he must have been, alone. Alone for a while in the modest home that he struggled to make for my sister and I. It saddens me very deeply.

All I thought of in 1946 was going to a new country, new horizons, and new people. Though she was living with Daddie, Mamie was busy with her own life, with new friends, sometimes bringing one or two of them home to meet Daddie. They were not exactly his cup of tea, but he said nothing. Only now that I have come a long way on this earthly journey, do I realize how much we can hurt, without meaning to, those who are the closest to us when we are very young.

Allan, shortly after our wedding was sent to the Canadian Embassy in Paris. He wrote many letters and there were many phone calls. At one point he broke his right wrist while cranking a jeep, he still continued to write, with his left hand.

His letters told me of the chaps he worked with; he described favourite restaurants and cafés, Notre Dame Cathedral, the Louvre, and many other places of interest in Paris. He told me working for Canadian Ambassador, George Vanier, was very fulfilling. Watching Vanier many years later on television when he became the Governor General of Canada, I would see what a very special person he was, as was Madame Vanier, and their son, Paul. They were a very special family with goodness seemingly emanating from all of them.

Allan said he liked Paris, but for him, it didn't compare to London. I think it was Sir Christopher Wren who said, "When one is tired of London, one is tired of living."

In no time at all, or so it seemed, Allan was sent back to Canada. We only saw one another briefly for a few hours before he left.

One day I got a letter telling me that during his medical discharge examination, they found his blood pressure to be very, very high. He would need surgery to treat the condition; the sympathetic nerves would be operated on near the kidneys. It was a new operation and had never been done in Calgary before, the surgeons would never attempt it on anyone over twenty-five, which meant Allan was the right age. (This operation is not performed any more as it is now considered too dangerous. The conditions are now controlled with drugs). This news was quite a blow, but when we are young, from somewhere, possibly from up above, we are given the wherewithal to weather most storms, and prayers don't do any harm.

*Allan on 8th Avenue in Calgary just after
he returned to Canada.*

A new experience for me, Allan's truly extended family.
I'm on the far right.

Another something new that came along much later —
baseball on the prairie.

Chapter 6

Prairie Adjustments

April 15th, 1947, the day I arrived in Calgary. Just six days earlier we had docked in Halifax, Nova Scotia, and now we were hundreds of railway miles across Canada in the province of Alberta. We had sailed across the Atlantic in the Cunard liner, *Aquitania*, without incident. The food on the *Aquitania*, and for that matter, the food on the train across Canada, was so different from our wartime rations. The bread was so white and after years of eating our grey English loaves, it was miraculous. There was always something to eat in England in the war years, but I felt quite spoiled and pampered with the delicious food on the ship and train.

Crossing the Atlantic and crossing Canada, I wondered what Allan's family would be like, as they must have wondered about me.

Allan was there to meet me at the railway station, as were his mother and father, and younger brother Bernie, seventeen years old. I was one of the last of the British war brides to finally reach her Canadian husband.

I noticed Allan didn't look too well and he had lost some weight. He was soon to go into the hospital for the first operation, and as this was the first time it had been done in Calgary, naturally he was anxious.

We went from the railway station to their bright little family home. It was well kept, nothing elaborate. Later that same day, in order to be alone together, Allan and I went for a walk. I especially remember that wonderful bright, sunny, afternoon that Allan and I walked the prairies and meadow larks were singing. I didn't remember meadow larks in England. There were gophers peeping out of their holes, and of course, I never saw any gophers in London.

The Glory Of The Dawn
by *Jacqueline O'Neill Dahm*

Oh! The Glory of the dawn,
Upon the mild and dewy morn'.
It really takes my breath away,
The splendour of the breaking day.

You'll never know what beauty is,
You'll never know the bliss.
You have to look upon this scene,
To know its beauty, so serene.

Then you'll hear the birdies sing,
For they're so thrilled with everything.
The fields, the trees, and lovely skies,
But best of all – the glorious sunrise.

I judged Allan's parents to be quite conservative, or I should say, reserved. I thought his mother took her job as a homemaker quite seriously, and his father, who was a salesman for a fruit company, was hard working. I learned much later that this poor chap had never earned more than two hundred dollars a month in his whole working life.

Allan's brother, Bernie, seemed to be cheery, a little chubby, but he was friendly and interested. He didn't look anything like Allan; he was dark with brown eyes, whereas Allan was fair with blue eyes. Later on as they grew older, it was easier to see that they were brothers.

Allan's father always came home for lunch, when the whole family sat together as they did for dinner at night, and Grace was always said. It seemed a well ordered family. In time I was to meet his grandparents, and numerous aunts and uncles, cousins and in-laws.

There was no television back then. Allan's father loved his radio, it seemed when he was home, the radio was always on. I remember so well the early evening comedies we listened to on the radio, *Amos and Andy, Jack Benny, Fibber Magee and Molly, Edgar Bergen and Charlie McCarthy*. These programmes would be on while we were having dinner on Sunday, a great source of entertainment.

There was a lot of visiting back and forth to the homes of Allan's relatives. Surprise parties were put on for me and I don't remember being too happy about them, I wasn't too delirious when I had to be at a certain aunt's place, and I would say to Allan, "I would rather not go." But Allan explained its importance, and when I got there, they were all sitting in the dark, the lights went on, and they would shout, "surprise." It was a shower. I'd never heard of such a thing before. The only showers I knew were April showers, rain showers, snow showers. We didn't have this custom in England.

Allan's brother played the violin, and quite well too. He had been playing since he was six years old. He taught violin at Mount Royal College, and was also in the Calgary symphony orchestra as concert meister of the first violins. The orchestra may have been called Mount Royal Symphony Orchestra at that time. We went to the concerts, and they were enjoyable.

We also went to a few of the productions by the drama group in Calgary, *Workshop 14*. I remember how well they did *Night Must Fall* by Emlyn Williams.

* * *

Allan was admitted to the Colonel Belcher Hospital and had the first operation as was indicated necessary by his blood pressure. His parents and I visited Allan in intensive care and it was sad to see him so changed. He once weighed one hundred and eighty pounds, but he seemed to lose weight rapidly. The doctors were not optimistic, and certainly we weren't, he looked so ill.

After many anxious weeks, Allan began to show improvement, very slowly. The doctors said he would soon be allowed to go to the convalescent unit, but it would be at least three months before the second operation. We saw as much as we could of one another in those days, although taking busses was an effort for him. I believe the doctors wondered, "What have we done to that poor boy." We wanted nothing more than the time to pass, the second operation over and finished with, so that he could start back on the final road to recovery. The time did pass, slowly but surely.

The second operation was a long one. Complications, infections, pleurisy, added to that, Allan was very low in spirit. We all started our daily trips to the hospital again and it was such a long time before Allan finally began to improve.

When he was finally allowed out of the hospital to the convalescent unit, he weighed about ninety pounds. His times in the hospital and convalescent unit were spread over a full year. How relieved we were when he was finally discharged from the convalescent unit, but it was a long, long, time before he was back to his normal weight of one hundred and eighty pounds.

In May of 1948 I received a letter from Mamie telling me that our Father had died the day after her birthday on May 18th. A sad day indeed and I hadn't even been able to say goodbye! Maybe those close to us know our thoughts. I hope so.

A brighter occurrence in October of that year, our daughter, Theresa Anne was born at 1:10 a.m. on the 26th, she weighed six pounds, twelve and a half ounces, was nineteen inches long. Complete in every detail, just the way babies are supposed to look, pink, white, gold and very blue eyes! Now we were three!

Allan was very worried wondering how he could make a living for us. Rushing into the army at seventeen, he had had no time to train for anything. He took an accounting course at a Calgary secretarial school and when finished, he said he felt well enough to look for a job. He still wasn't back to his normal weight, nor to his former health, but he had come a long way.

*Proud Daddy Allan with his first born daughter Theresa Anne
in Bowness Park.*

And Mummy with Terrie, the same day in the park.

He quickly landed a job with an oil company, and liked the job, and they seemed quite pleased with him. He had been working there a few weeks when he discovered that they had neglected to have him take the standard medical at the time he applied for the job. Sadly, he didn't pass the medical; they had to let him go.

He was quite down about this, but it wasn't long before he was engaged as the accountant at a well-known men's wear store in Calgary. All was going well until he was asked to clean the washroom, and he told them, "I'm an accountant, I'm not a janitor." So that didn't work out. Once again the hunt was on.

At that time, we were living in a tiny little house that belonged to Allan's parents, their first home as they started life together. Our finances didn't run to a telephone and there was no plumbing therein, but there was a cold water tap in the little kitchen, and a stone sink. The house had a living room, and a tiny bedroom. Allan and his brother had started to work on a bathroom, but it never did get finished. Like many houses on the prairies in those days, there was a privy at the back. At that time, there was still a lot of prairie around in Calgary.

One lovely summer's day in 1949 the neighbour's daughter came running over to tell Allan he was wanted on the phone. Allan came back from the neighbour's house full of excitement. He was to go for an interview with the Sheriff at the Calgary Court House.

"When do you go?" I asked him.

"I have to be there in an hour and a half," he replied.

He made sure to put on his best suit; actually, it was his only suit, one that he had bought when he returned from overseas. With all of the medical happenings in between, the least of his worries had been clothing. However, he remembered something his dad had told him, "Always have a good shine on your shoes, because even if your clothes aren't the most expensive, if they are clean and neat, and there is a shine on your shoes, you'll make a good impression." I must say he looked good as he left for the bus.

I could hardly wait 'til he came back with his news and was sitting outside waiting for him to return. It was unnecessary to ask the question, "Did you get the job?" as he came through the gate. He was beaming all over.

"So when do you start?" I asked.

"I start tomorrow," he said. "They are in dire need of an accountant."

He took to the job so easily and they all seemed to take to him, and there was no need to pass a medical.

"You know what," he said at the end of his first day there, "we only work half days in July and August."

Prairie Sunrise.

The Rocky Mountains.

Chapter 7

Home, Where The Heart Is

Soon Allan's dad sold the little house, so we rented a basement suite that was nothing more than one very large room. It did have a sink in it with hot and cold water, but no fridge or stove. We had our own little Acme stove, and there was an icebox we used in the outer basement but I don't think we ever bought any ice.

The couple we rented from had a Great Dane dog, he weighed about one hundred and fifty or one hundred and sixty pounds, his name was Thor. The outer basement was his private toilet, making it an unpleasant task to use the stairs to go out, or use the bathroom upstairs. Renting such miserable quarters these days would be entirely against the law, breaking all of the health and sanitation rules. We didn't stay there any longer than we had to. I was sorry to leave our landlady, Lucy, for she was quite a delightful girl, but I didn't feel quite the same about her spouse.

The next place we called home went by the elegant name of 'Deer Lodge'. In its heyday it must have been quite a lovely home and the owners would have been financially substantial. The floors were hardwood throughout. To say it had seen better days would be quite an understatement. Our furnished room there consisted of a brass bed with a badly sagging spring, a very old rocking chair, a big old chest of drawers, and a table that was very ancient, only big enough to hold two plates and two cups and saucers. There was no covering on the hardwood floors, not even a strip of carpet by the side of the bed. But I must say that the man who owned the house was a likeable person, even though the sheets he provided us with were not much wider than bandages. There were no cooking facilities in this room and no fridge. We used a hot plate for any cooking that we did.

Deer Lodge was a three storey house with two or three rooms rented on each floor, with one bathroom on each floor, shared by the tenants. One day I left my wedding ring in the bathroom and when I went back for it, it wasn't there. I could only assume that one of the other renters had taken it, which distressed me terribly. It was the most beautiful wedding ring I have ever seen, made of platinum with a ten-sided design, alternating between one side being plain, the next featuring a chipped diamond therein.

One Saturday mid-morning there were loud voices on the landing outside our door. The landlord was telling the girls that rented the room next door, in no uncertain terms, that they were not welcome there. He was in the process of putting their suitcases in the hall and they were screaming their protests at him. The girls were ladies of the evening and we had had no idea that this was their profession.

Not too long after this incident, the landlord, who was not in very good health, sold the place to a woman who made many elaborate promises to the tenants. She was going to renovate the whole house, make a wonderful suite for us, or so she said. The suite would take in our room, the one the girls had had, which was a very large room, and part of the landing. This would give us two bedrooms, a bathroom, a kitchen and a living room and she would also renovate the sun porch for us. All of this was just pipe dreams. None of it ever happened and she turned out to be a real battleaxe, but we did have some very memorable times in Deer Lodge.

One day, as I stood on the stoop hanging out my baby's laundry, I heard someone say in rather a cracked voice, "Hello Mrs." I turned and nearly fell off the stoop when I saw a middle-aged woman who had either been in an accident or someone had done her a mischief about the face, for her nose was broken and several front teeth were missing. This coupled with her strange voice, did not make for the best first impression, but she and her husband became good friends of Allan and I. We had some very good times with them. We later learned that her brother had hit Helen in the face with a shovel when she was ten years old. I guess it would be very hard to avoid a broken nose and missing teeth if that happened to one.

The couple lived in the basement of the house. Above them was a very large family who occupied two or three rooms. There was an ongoing "war" between the couple and the large family. When either thought the other was making too much noise, they'd stamp with work boots on the floor above and in the basement they'd knock on the ceiling with a broom. Sometimes the doors would open and they would hurl rude remarks at one another. It was quite funny to observe.

We had no stove but our friends in the basement had one. They said any time we wanted anything cooked, they would be glad to do it for us. I thought it would be nice to have a good English roast beef dinner and Yorkshire pudding, so took it down to them. But that poor soul, Helen, had no idea how to cook, none. It was terribly sad what happened to that much anticipated roast beef dinner. It was very ugly. We couldn't determine what was supposed to be the Yorkshire and what was supposed to be the gravy, it all looked so grey, but our friends meant well, and that was all that mattered.

Fred, Helen's husband, turned a hand to anything to make a living. He had a booth at the Calgary Stampede where he sold hot dogs and hamburgers. At Christmas time he sold Christmas trees and he did rough carpentry, he was no finisher, but he did the best he could. Later on in this story I will touch on Fred's tenure in the real estate business adding to the colourful characters and events that happened at this house while we lived there.

I must mention Mary and John who came from Bienfait, Saskatchewan, 'Bean Fate', as they called it. Allan was at work. He'd been at the Court House a couple of weeks. It was mid-morning when there was a knock at the door. A very pleasant woman appeared when I said, "Come in." She was holding a very pretty dress. She wanted me to try it on to see if it would fit her daughter. When I asked what size it was, she said it was size sixteen. I said, "Well,

I'm only a six or an eight, there is no way I could tell you if it would fit your daughter or not." I rather think that was just an excuse for her to get to know us. She said, "You want a cup of tea, Mrs.?" I detected an accent. I learned later she was Métis, and her husband John, was a Swede. They too became our very good friends.

I had tea with Mary in her room that was in happy disarray and I could see that she had been playing the 'a-cord-dean' as she called it in the midst of this confusion. She made a delightful cup of tea which she served with *Kitkat* bars, and while I was there, she sat on her glasses! This happened more than once in our friendship. She said she was waiting for their 'fornitures'. She was also waiting for her husband John and her daughter Theresa. She hoped they were coming the following weekend. John was a finishing carpenter.

Allan and I spent many a pleasant evening with Helen and Fred and Mary and John in our respective rooms, and we gathered that John had had to work quite early in his life and didn't have the advantage of a lot of education. He learned in the school of hard knocks.

We can't leave Deer Lodge without telling of our time with Tiny. Tiny was also from Bienfait, Saskatchewan, and a friend of Mary and John's. He was six foot six and he weighed over two hundred and fifty pounds. He came one day to Calgary, swinging a goose by the neck. He wore overalls, no jacket and rubbers and no socks. It was chilly for it was nearing Christmas.

Mary and John didn't know that he was coming, he just arrived! Tiny knew that he would be welcomed without question, as Mary and John welcomed anyone they knew from out of town, taking care of them for a night or two. Tiny also knew, that Mary would 'cook his goose'! The dinner that Mary cooked on a hot plate was nothing short of miraculous. She cooked the goose and a couple of ducks and all the fixings solely on the hot plate, and there was dessert and beverages aplenty. Mary had been a cook in a lumber camp. Tiny was feeling quite happy, declining food for a while, 'cos he didn't want to spoil his glow. He didn't have too much difficulty eating most of his 'Christmas goose', even with his glow!

Soon after this we moved to Fifth Avenue North West, not too far from Louise Bridge and near the Crystal swimming pool. There was a laundry nearby that had to take down its controversial sign, and rightly so, that showed a coloured lady bent over a wash tub. Although we left Deer Lodge behind us, we kept in touch with our friends.

We were quite near to town in this new location and Allan and I weren't sure of the wisdom of this move. Rent of sixty-five dollars a month was a far cry from the previous twenty-four dollars a month. It *was* quite a strain on our meagre finances, but we managed.

The place had a very large kitchen, and a bathroom containing both a bath and a basin. Adjacent to the bathroom was the toilet which would not be approved by sanitation and building codes today for there must be running water where the toilet is to meet hygiene standards. The living room was a decent size, a large bedroom and a smaller one, and there was also quite a bit of landing space. Added to all of this luxury, we were completely self-contained. We had our own front door, and I must say, we enjoyed a lot more privacy.

The owners of the house allowed that we might use a portion of the garden to grow whatever we wished. We did try to grow a garden there but it was not too successful, our runner bean crop produced one runner bean about eighteen inches long!

While we were living there we had another little girl, Janine Allison, born on the 14th of September 1950. She weighed six pounds, eight ounces, was also eighteen inches long! Very blonde - very dear.

Our very nice English neighbour, who had been a nurse in the First World War, would ask me to tea quite often. I would take my babies with me, and she just doted on them. She had grandchildren, but they were in Edmonton, so she liked to pretend that my children were *her* grandchildren. She was very good to me and my children. She didn't even scold Janine when she pulled at the table

91

Janine Allison in the wild prairie grass.

Ragamuffins, growing like weeds on the prairie, Terrie and Janine.

cover where her plants were, but she told me she didn't smile at her!

Things were going along quite well and we were able to take care of the rent, though we had to be quite thrifty. We made friends with some of the other Court House employees and their wives, and socialized with them. Time moved along quite quickly.

The chicken house, fixed up a little.

The entrance to the old basement, the Model A Ford,
and the rundown chicken house with Janine and Terrie.

Chapter 8

On The River Bank

One evening Helen and Fred came to call, our friends from Deer Lodge. Fred had gone into real estate and told us that there was a piece of property for sale, an acre and a half, located on the Bow River in Shouldice Park. He thought it might just be the thing for us.

As the evening was still quite light, we went to see it right away. It was a nice piece of property. The house that was originally there had burned down, but there was a good size chicken house on the land. I said to Allan we could fix that place up and live in it until we built a proper house. "We can't live in there," he said, "it's just a chicken house." I'm quite sure people have lived in a lot worse places. After removing the dead chicken from therein, fix it up is exactly what we did. We lived there for five years until we built a proper house.

We had no money; we were just starting out, no savings account, or anything like that. The price of the property on the Bow River was twenty-five hundred dollars. It might just have well have been twenty-five thousand dollars. Allan did have a job though and that was something in our favour. He went to one bank and managed to get a thousand dollar loan. I went to another, and managed to get a fifteen hundred dollar loan. We had many anxious moments. How to pay this tremendous loan back. I think Someone above must have been watching over us, because we did it.

I don't think Allan was quite back to his full strength yet, but he did services for the sheriff, did some moving with an uncle of his, stacked shelves at the Bay, and did gyprocing. The two of us cleaned offices so the debt might be cleared off speedily.

95

When Allan came home, sometimes as late as ten o'clock at night, we'd work on the chicken house, and we did manage to make it into a cozy little home. I wonder how many men, even in the best of health, would be willing to do all this to make a home for their families? He was a very good man.

During this time the building of our house was going steadily forward. Allan helped with this also, in addition to all the extra jobs he was doing. This was a stipulation of the Veteran's Land Act, that the veteran share in the work of the building of the house.

One night we were working on the part we called the end room, putting gyproc sheets on the ceiling. Allan would secure one end to the ceiling while I held the other end. At one point he was quick to notice that my end was moving. I had fallen asleep and the gyproc was sliding out of my grip, and if it hadn't been for Allan's quick action, I would have crashed right through the window. Needless to say, the work stopped for that evening.

Most of the materials that went into renovating that little house came to us through Allan's ingenuity. When they were turning the old Court House into a museum, there was a lot of scrap material to be had, like battleship linoleum we used on the floors, and masonite that we used for the ceilings. From somewhere he managed to get damaged gyproc sheets which we used on the walls. There was the used lumber he got from a Mr. Miller for a very minimal cost. I think our biggest expense must have been the paint we used to brighten up the little house as it became more finished.

Allan's dad found us a front door that had quite a bit of glass in it, it cost about six dollars. Some cousins of Allan's gave us a stoop so that we would have a front step.

Court House friends lent us an old coal and wood stove. I did cook a few roasts in it and managed to bake a few cakes that turned out quite well. We gathered our wood on the nearby prairies and river banks. We had a Model A Ford at that time which we had bought for $100.00. Allan would drive to Littlewood's Coal Merchants in Calgary -

weigh the Model A - then fill it with coal and weigh it again! Oft times there wasn't time to unload it before Allan left for work. Our evenings were always very full, so he would just leave me a bucket of coal and off to work with the rest still in the Model A. Many a chuckle we had about his being the modern day Scrooge, so miserly with the coal. In reality, he was quite the opposite!

A friend put the electrical wiring in for us. Allan put the gas line in, city wouldn't approve it, even though Allan had done a perfect job, 'til the plumbing and heating man gave it the okay. At that time there was no bathroom in the former chicken house. There was a privy at the back about two hundred feet or so from the little house, and in the very cold weather, we had to use potties and buckets and things, and emptying buckets I suppose was just about Allan's most unfavourite job.

We still had our little Acme stove and we had an old icebox, but we only filled it with ice once or twice. We acquired a fridge after a little while. It was one of those deals put together for the very vulnerable. "Bring us your old hat, bring us your old coat, anything, we'll give you a hundred dollars towards a new fridge." I suppose in our very young days, we were very trusting and very vulnerable, but thank goodness, we do, and we did learn, one or two things along life's way.

After Allan put the gas in the little house, we gave the coal and wood stove back to our friends and we did miss its comforting heat. For a while that little Acme stove was the sole heat and cooking source in the little house, we put the oven and the burners on and we were quite comfortable. We left the end room door closed so we wouldn't have to heat that, for we were not using it yet, we were still renovating it. I remember how Allan's parents worried about us using that little stove, for they weren't sure if Allan had vented it right, but he certainly had. They used to come and check on us at odd times to make sure we were all right.

Allan had made a little bedroom for the girls in between the end room and the very large living-cum-kitchen-cum-hide-a-bed area that Allan and I used. It was the cutest little room. He cut out two window areas but did not glass them in, making a fairly wide shelf on the bottom. I remember the girls had big fat piggy banks on those shelves. Terrie had a pink one, Janine had a blue one, and there were other things they put on the shelves, I can't remember now, but I do remember the piggies. I think Allan's parents brought them back from the United States on one of their visits.

The room faced onto the front door and there was also a good sized window to the left of the door, so they did have quite a bit of natural light, and there was electric light, of course. We bought two youth beds for them and two very small chests of drawers, and two small rocking chairs. It did make a very nice little room for them, complete with the addition of a little heater.

We felt like early pioneers. Actually, that's just what we were, latter day pioneers. We moved to that little chicken house in 1952. The years we spent there were good years with many happy memories. In those early years our taxes went to the village of Montgomery and they were very minimal, I think about seventeen dollars a year. When we first moved to that little house we were supplied water by our neighbours, but it wasn't long before Allan got the existing well working.

In those days, backyard fires were allowed and everyone enjoyed the fireside fun down by the river. We'd roast wieners and potatoes in the fire and marshmallows and there was always plenty of coffee to go around. We had a Court House gathering at one time where the girls played the boys in baseball. The girls lost dismally but it was all in fun, there was a barbecue afterwards. Allan and Frank, another Court House friend, and a former pilot in the R.A.F. in World War II, joined the police auxilliary. Frank and his wife, Nella, became our very good friends and there were many barbecues subsequent to that.

To cheer up dull days when the girls couldn't play outside, I spread a blanket on the floor and we'd have a picnic, and of course, the dolls were also invited. A favourite summer pastime of the girls and I was sitting on

Terrie, down by the river.

The swings that Allan built.

the river bank with our feet in the water throwing stones in the river and watching the ever widening circles they made. As the house was very small and didn't take a lot of care, there was time for these pleasant interludes. Allan built swings for the girls in the backyard and I remember very vividly the day of January 18th, 1954. Terrie and Janine were swinging in those swings and they had summer dresses on, so there must have been a Chinook blowing.

I never felt bad about our humble home. We had goals and knew we were going to reach them. In 1954 Terrie started at the Catholic school. She'd only been there a few days when an older girl brought her home, then I felt bad, but only for her, not for myself. I suppose I wondered if she was embarrassed and ashamed of her modest home! Allan's dad soon straightened out the problem. He was paying his taxes to the separate school board and he let them know his granddaughters had a right to be at the Catholic school. Our taxes, minimal as they were, were going to the village of Montgomery.

Many's the time relatives and friends would come to help with the work on the house. These occasions often turned into social hours after a while, but they always got something done, and the times were pleasant that we spent together.

Summers in the little house seemed endless. That property was a beautiful spot for our children to grow up, an acre and a half of playground and their own special places, including the river bank. We had no fears for *their* safety there, for they had been well schooled in the dangers of the river. Only when little friends came to play did we get anxious. There was very little traffic on Thirteenth Avenue in those days. This was long before the Community Centre went in, before the swimming pool and the sports complex. These were all eventually located, as was our property, in Shouldice Park.

It didn't take the girls very long to make friends with the identical twin girls next door. In their growing up years they were always together, and their family was included in many of our social activities. Lesley and Gailene were a little

100

under a year younger than Janine and a little under two years younger than Terrie. They later were to form their own little club, and of course, Terrie was the president. We put up a little BA tent for the girls, inside were a little table and chairs and rugs on the ground. The girls liked to eat their lunch in the tent and sometimes the twins would join them.

We were the first ones in our immediate area to get a television set and the first in the family. Sometimes neighbours would drop in to watch it and oft times Allan's parents and grandparents. These were the days of black and white television. How we looked forward to Ed Sullivan's, *Toast of the Town*. Television was erratic with little regular programming. We used to watch the patterns, hoping something would come on. However, there was always something for the kids on Saturday mornings and the twins would come over to watch with our girls. What a long way television has come since those years.

Christmas 1954, the first television set
on Thirteenth Avenue, Janine and Terrie
and Gram's hand!

101

*The girls and a neighbour's dog
all boxed in.*

Ready for the prairie tricycle Grand Prix.

Saturday was shopping day. It wasn't always easy in the winter getting the shopping back home. The driveway was about seven hundred feet long, often we had to leave the Model A at the top of the driveway if snow had covered the trail, and put the shopping on the toboggan to get it to the house. It was quite the caper chasing cans and packages in the snow. It wasn't always nature that wrecked the trail. Sometimes tradesmen, relatives and friends, would come blundering down the trail without due caution, wrecking the perfect trail that Allan had built. At these times, Allan was more than a little angry and said words not repeatable here.

Saturday night was steak night in the little place and we peeled potatoes and mashed them, they seemed to be everyone's favourite, with the steak and peas.

By the fall of 1956 the work on the new house was continuing to go very well. We were lucky to have the

Getting ready to dig the foundation for the new house on Thirteenth. Gram in the bucket.

interest and the help of a certain Mr. B, a Veteran's Land Act building inspector. He would take us around to various lumber yards, plumbing supplies, carpenters, and get the best prices for us. Maybe we knew just how to take him, he was quite the character, and he told us in his Cockney accent, that the "chimlee" had to be such-and-such high and "them joists" had to be just so and he talked of the "perime'er" of the house. Some of the Vets didn't fare as well as we did, though when he told them," that chimlee don't look right," and, "be'er come down," and at some places, he was ordered off the property, once with a shotgun. I asked him once or twice for dinner - "You sure you go' enuf," he said. I have to smile when I think of him, and I think of him quite warmly.

Janine started school, what a big day it was for her. Fortunately, there was none of the mix-up we had when Terrie started school, and we told Terrie she must take care of Janine and bring her home safely. The big thing on Janine's birthday was she had her birthday in the new house. It wasn't quite ready to move into yet, but she did have her birthday there.

New Year 1957 - I cooked my first turkey in that little Acme stove. It was so big, I couldn't shut the oven door properly and I was amazed that it turned out so well. Allan's parents joined us and we had a very pleasant day to start the New Year.

We had lived in the former chicken house for over four years. It served us well, kept us sheltered and warm. We no longer had to attack the grass with the grass whip. We had acquired a lawn mower, a much-needed item for there was a lot of grass on the riverside property.

We had put in a vegetable garden the second year, which flourished in subsequent years. There were many flowers planted by the previous owners, perennials that came back every year, the old fashioned kind, monkshood, delphiniums, Jerusalem cross, gypsophelia, tiger lilies, columbine, marguerites, all in abundance when we bought the property in '52.

Allan in the more-than-we-needed vegetable garden.

The vegetable garden did very well. It yielded a lot more than we could possibly use, so we were able to share with relatives and friends. Many hours were spent digging the crab grass from the area. One year we put in willow branches as stakes for the peas, but they didn't want to be stakes, they wanted to be little bushes, for they started to sprout. We planted some night scented stock right near our little place; sadly, it is not one of the showier flowers, but the fragrance it gave off in the evening was simply delightful. I remember throwing seeds with abandon in another patch we had cleared of the crab grass and they made a beautiful showing.

Even though some of our favourite times on Thirteenth Avenue were in the fall, I always found fall ineffably sad and still do, 'cos everything is dying, and soon winter comes to cover everything with it's white blanket! The fall was always a special time, gathering in the good things the garden had given us. We would have fires down by the river, bake potatoes and corn right in the fire, wieners and always marshmallows for the kids.

We put the potatoes from the garden on the grass to dry before putting them in sacks and storing them in the 'old basement' as we called the partial basement that was under the original house that had burned down. We didn't have a root cellar, but the old basement served quite well for storing the garden goodies.

In late fall the snow fence would go up, as the driveway was very long and we had to do what we could to prevent it being snowed in.

The water pump in the old basement was not in full working order when we bought the property, but not too long after we moved there, Allan got it working. He covered the old basement over with a concrete platform, installed a stand pipe with a faucet, so we didn't have to go to the neighbour's for water any more, and that large platform became the foundation of the family room that was added to the house many years later.

The new house ready for us to move in, as recently drawn by son Christopher.

One tremendous undertaking Allan completed in 1957 was to finish the work the tractor had begun for the septic field. I remember his digging trenches and filling them with gravel. Sometimes he would come in exhausted and perspiring, needing something sweet for quick energy, and I would make him two or three sandwiches of peanut butter and jam and he would drink several cups of tea.

October 1957, at last, it was the day for moving into the new house. Everything was finished in every detail. There were hardwood floors throughout except for the bathroom and the kitchen. How happy we were to have indoor plumbing, hot and cold water, and how we appreciated the bathtub. The following may sound a little prim, I think it is very good to have to work and wait for something, for then you can really appreciate it, and we certainly did! We didn't have a big housewarming, Allan's parents came and we celebrated having our first meal together in the new house. Relatives and friends and neighbours came by to show an interest in our new home.

We had a cat called Pip ...

… and a cat named Ming-Toy
that wouldn't go to bed without his pajamas.

We had a cat called Pip. Her full name was Pippin. She was a beautiful cat, a grey Persian with green eyes. She came from a bank where one of Allan's cousins worked. The bank cat had produced kittens, and she was one of the litter. She wasn't a very affectionate cat, but she was quite attached to Allan. She would sleep on his slippers when he was away at work. Of course, she moved with us to the new house.

We thought it would be nice to get a dog. The Thompson's, neighbours who also lived on Thirteenth Avenue, raised Springer Spaniels. It was Christmas time and Allan said he would get me one of the puppies for a Christmas present, so the four of us went down to the Thompson's to look over the puppies. The litter was old enough to leave the mother. Dollie, the mother, was a liver and white Springer, and she was a very good mother to her babies. Some of the puppies took after their mother in colouring and there were some black ones with white on them, but there was one that was all black. He seemed a little bigger than the others, and he was the one we picked out. I already had a name for him. I called him Nicholas Nickleby, as I always associate Dickens with Christmas. He was never called Nicholas, it was always Nickie.

Poor old Nickie, I guess he was his own worst enemy, for he didn't take kindly to anyone; tradesmen, paper boys, even relatives and friends. He didn't really want anyone around except the family. He loved his family dearly. I remember asking one of the twins, Gailene, if she liked Nickie. She said, "I like him when he's tired." He wasn't aggressive at these times. He grew into a very handsome dog, a very strong dog, but we could never break him of the habit of scaring people, and one day when he knocked the paper boy off his bike and tore his jeans, we thought it was time to send him away, and sadly, we did. We sent him away to a farm where they needed a good watchdog, and I hope he lived out his life very happily there. We were very sad to part with him.

Our first Christmas in the new house, Gram and Grampa joined us and Bernie was there too. The dinner turned out very well and I was very pleased with myself. All in all it was a good day. We played silly games and the folks left quite late in the evening. A very crisp evening and it was snowing lightly. On New Year's Eves we always woke the girls to toast the New Year in with a glass of ginger ale and Allan and I had something a little stronger. Traditionally, we went to Allan's parents on New Year's Day. It was also a tradition to go to the Hilton's, our next door neighbours, to toast the New Year with them, before we left for Gram and Grampa's. I remember Kay made a drink she called Angel Kisses, tho' when I left there, I thought they were more like velvet hammers. It was a good day at Allan's parents home, there were other relatives there, so it was quite a social time and the food was very good. The girls loved to go out visiting, especially Janine, and she still does to this day. But Terrie, Muff-Anne as she is now called, is more of a homebody.

1958. Hard to realize it was nearly six years since we had bought the river property. We had paid off the debt to the banks, and we had come quite a long way. We added things to the home and even managed some outside furniture. We were a little pleased with ourselves, but I hope not smug, for we still had a long way to go.

The girls were getting along fine in school, and making friends that they sometimes brought to the house for a sleep-over, but they still played a lot with the twins, Gailene and Lesley.

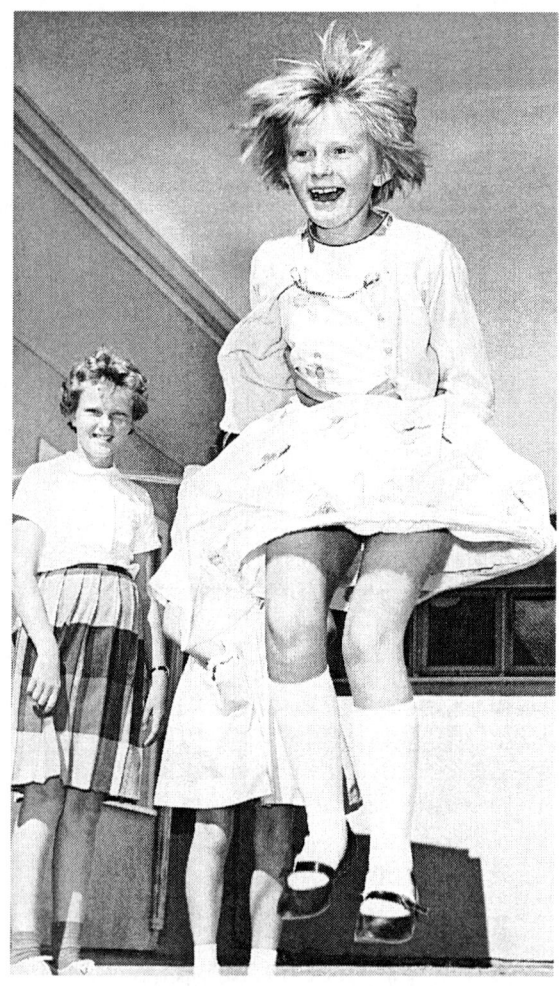

Janine at school, skipping during a recess.

This would have been the year that Terrie organized their little club. I gave them a fair sized area rug to put on the floor in a corner of the basement. They had some rocking chairs down there, a small table and some chairs. I think there was an old desk down there and an old chest of drawers. Terrie was the president. I think they had quite a bit of fun with their little club. They made a couple of picture books, and gave them to the Children's Hospital in Calgary. It was quite a caution to listen at the top of the stairs to their meetings. One time I heard Terrie make the motion, "We will now adjourn for refreshments," and Gailene, wanting to appear very knowledgeable said, "I object." What delightful girls the twins were and we did keep in touch for many years, 'til about five or six years ago. Another happy memory woven into the fabric of life.

Allan was doing very well at the Court House. He had been there going on nine years and learning a lot about the workings of the law.

He hadn't been at the Court House long before he was voluntarily handling the work of the Credit Union. In those years - it was a much smaller organization, today; they have their own suite of offices.

We had a lot of company once we were in the new house, and Allan was still doing extra jobs, for the Alberta government didn't pay princely wages. There had been raises over the years, but we never felt that we could go wild, so we were still quite careful. We didn't have time to get bored, and time moved along very swiftly.

That year we purchased a sand coloured Hillman Minx automobile. How excited we were. It had been repossessed from a chap who had quite a few aliases and I guess he wasn't making payments on it, so his misfortune was our gain. Sometimes the car would be so packed when Allan would drive to work it couldn't hold another person, for he would be driving the girls to school, and sometimes there would be three or four neighbours in the car also, for he didn't like saying no to anyone.

Sunday best and the Hillman Minx.

Allan and the Hillman Minx in his
not so Sunday best.

Janine joined the Brownies that year and thoroughly enjoyed all of their activities, but this was not for Terrie, it didn't appeal to her. She was very interested in art and very good at it. A few years later she took a course in Chinese art. Janine learned to play the recorder, and later came second in the Alberta Music Festival. They both took dance lessons from a local girl, and singing lessons from Miss Lumbers, and their little group put on shows at the local recreation centre, and they were entertaining.

The girls went to Camp Cadicasu that summer. They seemed to like it and enjoyed the camp activities. Allan and I went to see them a couple of times during the week that they were there, worrying about how they were getting on their first time away from home. It seemed we'd only just got the girls back from camp and it was time to start school again for another year.

Halloween leopards and
his majesty Ming-Toy.

A snoozing Janine with a beer bottle placed by humourous parental guidance!

Terrie and her first missing tooth.

Chapter 9

Growing Up

Fall was fast approaching. Time seemed to be flying by like the wind. School was going along very well for the girls and Allan's work at the Court House filled with accomplishment. Before we knew it, we were in the midst of Christmas preparations, and one evening Bernie phoned and talked to Allan. Their father had had a heart attack and died instantly, a very sad time for the family, just two weeks before Christmas.

Allan's mother was with us for Christmas and it was hard to see her facing her recent loss, but with the passage of time, things did get easier. She started to attend bingo again, as well as bowling. Later that winter she again began to become interested in her special TV shows. She always liked to see things coming back to life in the garden after their long winter's sleep, which gave her new hope that coming spring.

As 1959 dawned, we realized that we had been on the property for seven very good years. Years of work inside, outside, landscaping added, furniture, and general improvements. We had felt like the king of the castle when our finances allowed us a patio umbrella.

Many were the happy times spent with family and friends inside and outside the property on Thirteenth Avenue. A lot more people could be accommodated outside, but they did seem to flow over into the house as well. There certainly was no time to get bored as there was always something going on; parent-teacher meetings, school activities. And we were glad we had the nice house to entertain them in. Gram was with us a lot on weekends and holidays and when she wasn't with us, she was with Lorraine and Bernie.

When we first moved into the new house in '57, we established a custom of having our relatives and friends in for Boxing Day. We would also have a New Year's gathering, a custom that lasted for quite a few years.

Another one of our favourite times, and one of Gram's too, was driving to Bragg Creek or to Okotoks on a Sunday. We would take along a large thermos of coffee, some orange juice, or punch, for the girls. There would be wieners and marshmallows to roast over the campfire. Not really a regular picnic, but just a little diversion from the every day. These pristine areas would be so especially beautiful in the fall; that they would make your heart ache. When we got home in the evening, we might have had a hot roast beef sandwich if we had been a little extravagant and got one of those meat packages from Leon the butcher on Tenth Street.

Allan and me, picnic Sundays at Bragg Creek.

Mermaid by the sea, Terrie at English Bay, Vancouver.

It was in August of this year, that Gram took Allan and I and the girls on vacation to Vancouver. It was a pleasant break for everyone. We stayed at a place called the Maxine Hotel. It wasn't too far from the ocean and the accommodation was quite adequate and pleasant. The girls and I would walk to the beach and have a little swim, while Gram and Allan were still sleeping. The girls would get quite anxious if I went too far out. On the way back from our outing, the girls would have chocolate milk and chips.

Cyril, one of Gram's brothers who had moved to Vancouver, came to see us with his friend Lil. We later made a date to have dinner with them at a mall, I think it was called the Oak Ridge Mall. Norman Johnson and his wife, Chris, came to see us at the Maxine. He worked at the Court House.

We did spend a lot of time on the beach in those halcyon days. We saw *Kismet* at the Theatre Under The Stars. Cyril and Lil were with us and she seemed to be quite a Dal Richards fan. We went to see Ben Hur starring a very young Charlton Heston, one of the movies made with a lot of new technology. I recall how very long it was.

Another item from my Vancouver memory bank is when we went to the Sylvia Hotel. The dinner was very good, all in all a very pleasant evening. As we were making our way onto the street, I missed the very steep step, tripped, and went galloping down the street at about fifty miles and hour. I don't think it was what I had to drink there, for all I had was tea, and the sling wasn't much stronger than the girls' Shirley Temples. I think I must have been prattling idly and not paying attention to what I was doing.

One evening the girls were playing in the yard of the hotel with a beach ball. There was a one-eyed cat in residence there, taking the air at that time, and very soon the beach ball was no more. I don't think the girls liked that one-eyed cat very much!

It was soon time to say goodbye to Vancouver, and I'm sure the sojourn there renewed our spirits and widened our horizons. A time well remembered, for this was our first real holiday. Heretofore we had one or two weekends in Banff with Allan's parents, and a few day trips there, and one very memorable camping trip in Coeur d'Alene, Idaho.

Relatives and friends had been encouraging us to take a little trip. In fact urging us to do so, saying we deserved it, even pressuring us to take their camping gear, and as we have never been much of the borrowing kind, we hesitated before accepting the offer of these dear people. But we should have been absolutely steadfast in refusing, for everything that could go wrong, went wrong, with the borrowed camping gear. During the trip someone tripped over the tent and tore it and we put holes in the sleeping bags and one of the air mattresses. Melting butter had left large grease stains on the tent. Even though we were able to get the sleeping bags invisibly mended, and the air mattress repaired at a service station. We had to take the tent to a tent and awning maker who repaired it and got *some* of the stain out of it. But I think that was one of life's most embarrassing moments for us when we had to return it all to the owners. We rather felt like throwing ourselves into a pit. Since that day, we vowed to borrow no more. Even to this day, if someone presses a book on me to read, or something to try out, I just return them after a while, knowing very well if I read the book or used the item, something disastrous will happen.

With all this reminiscing, I seem to have lost a year somewhere. On the 9th of August 1961, Allan was made Administrator of the Supreme and District Courts. He was now a Justice of the Peace, a Notary Public, and Commissioner for Oaths. I was pleased for him, but it did mean a heavier workload. In the winter of the previous year I started work in the office of Arden Sutherland. They were a plumbing and heating firm in Manchester. Not Manchester, England, but Manchester, a district in Calgary.

With all the comings and goings, hustle and bustle of family life, how could I not have mentioned those very special occasions when the girls made their First Communion.

Terrie made her First Communion in 1955. She was very excited and nervous too. I remember how dear and ·angelic all the children looked. The one that stands out in every mother's mind is, of course, her own child. And why do mothers cry at such times, possibly because it is a very emotional time. Allan's parents were in the church for the occasion. After Mass, the church and the school put on a little celebration for the communicants, we then spent the rest of the day at Allan's parents. The weather was very kind that day because I remember the girls re-enacting the whole ceremony outside in the garden. They were quite serious about it. We captured this on the black and white snaps we took that day.

Janine had her special day in 1957. Gram and Grampa were at the church and the sun was smiling down on all the dear little people. The little girls in their white dresses and the little boys in their white shirts and their navy blue blazers. This time the First Communicants were treated to a pancake breakfast at Smitty's Pancake House.

I'm sure they were all quite delighted, I know Janine was. We spent a pleasant afternoon in the garden at Gram and Grampa's and Gram cooked a special dinner in honour of the occasion.

We made it to 1962, the year that Janine competed in the Alberta Music Festival. She placed second in grades four, five and six, of the recorder. The adjudicators said many nice things about her playing but Allan and I thought she should have placed first.

This was the year that I took my first plane trip by returning to England for the first time since coming to Canada in 1947. It was nice to see my sister Mamie and her son and many of the old friends. The England I found was much changed from the England I left fifteen years before. It was a very full holiday, with so many emotions that seemed to be bumping into one another all at once; happiness, sadness, bewilderment, nostalgia, disappointment that you really didn't belong in that scenario any more. You were just an onlooker, a spectator, not part of it. I was to return again many times to the land where I was born, for one never loses this very deep attachment. Even though I am now a Canadian citizen, I never relinquished my British citizenship.

On my return to Canada a warm welcome awaited me at the Calgary Airport. Allan and the girls had decorated the house with 'welcome home' signs and I must say it did feel very good to be home again. The rest of the day seemed to be one of happy confusion with everybody talking at once.

So much had happened that year, Allan and I were married in St. Bernard's Church on March 10th. Father Gerharz performed the ceremony. Bertha and Leo were our witnesses and Gram was there also.

We had this second marriage ceremony sixteen years after we had been married by a Registrar in Paddington, a district of London, because the Catholic Church does not recognize civil ceremonies, so in the eyes of the Catholic Church we were not married, but we certainly were married according to Civil Law.

*Leo and Bertha, myself and Allan. This was the day we were
married "again". I am still in my wedding dress, Allan on
the other hand was quick to change out of his suit into
something more comfortable.*

Bertha made the dress for the occasion. We had a few
laughs about this. She would have Leo Junior try on the
dress, wearing Bertha's high heels when I wasn't there, for
he was just about the same size. He wasn't too keen about
doing this, but did it all with good humour, and Bertha
made a very good job of the dress.

We had a little celebration at the house afterwards.
We would have liked Harvey to come but he was too far
away at that time. Harvey was a family friend who was with
us for many celebrations. He started working with Allan at
the Court House when quite young. The girls looked very
pretty in their summery dresses. Terrie in pink, for that's

her favourite colour, and Janine in a very pretty pale green. Janine played her recorder and I know she was quite nervous and ill at ease with Father Gerharz there. All in all it was a good day, a happy day.

That year we were looking forward to a new arrival, hoping it would be a little boy, but sadly it was not to be and the loss was quite traumatic. The nuns at the Holy Cross Hospital said this might be nature's way or God's way of preventing an imperfection before it happened, and maybe why I miscarried. I was quite low in spirits for some time after this experience.

In October Terrie was fourteen, whereas Janine was twelve in September, and couldn't wait to catch up to her. Jessie and Gordon, old Court House friends, and their girls Stephanie and Shauna, came for the birthday dinner and as it was late October, the setting was Halloween. During the festivities, Shauna couldn't wait to tell us that Terrie and Stephanie were sharing a beer and I suppose she thought this was terribly wicked. Stephanie would have been a little older than Terrie.

Christmas and New Year meant a lot of company, family and friends visiting. We did miss our neighbour, dear old Bessie when we visited next door; she was such a good friend. Bessie left this place some time ago and Charlie hired a housekeeper to keep things in order for him.

For recreation we joined the Montgomery square dance group called, *The Melody Squares* along with neighbours Gwenneth and Art and Harvey. We stayed with them for quite a while and we did have a lot of fun. I remember Art commenting, "When one knows all there is to know about square dancing, it's no more fun." If this is true, we have years of fun ahead for us! We had a fling at the Scottish country dancing. We learned a few of the basics, but this group was not for us. *They* took the whole thing too seriously. They rather frowned on us and thought we were quite naughty, because *we* didn't take it seriously. Our dear old neighbour Derek who told us he was Scottish by adoption, took the whole thing seriously. He even took square dancing seriously. With all the dancing I've done, excluding ballet and tap dancing, ballroom, line dancing, pattern dancing and Latin dancing, I've found square dancing to be the happiest.

We signed up with the *Hypnosis Society of Alberta* which we found quite interesting. We learned quite a few things, met some interesting people, heard about dentists using hypnosis instead of freezing for some of their work. Some of the group were of the opinion it was quite hard to hypnotize someone with a short attention span. Derek joined the group, *Stepping Stone to Transcendental Meditation*, and to the best of my knowledge he is still involved with transcendental meditation today, teaching it, taking it all quite seriously.

I later joined the *Clarion Toastmistress Club of Calgary*. This also was a learning experience but I think they may have been unhappy with me 'cos I didn't take it seriously enough. But all the courses Allan and I took were in our spare time. We thought it best not to take anything too seriously, and enjoy it a little! I can even boast of getting the *Blarney Stones* a few times, large and small, while with the *Clarion*. The large one was given for Best Written Speech of the Evening, the small one for Best Extemporaneous Speech. I've never liked meetings, but I did find the *Toastmistress* experience made them a little less unpleasant.

I shan't leave the *Toastmistress* story without telling you about the party we had for one of the *Clarion* members, Betty, when she won the *District Toastmistress Competition*. There must have been more than forty *Toastmistresses* in our rumpus room that night from *Clarion*, but there were one or two members of other clubs. Allan and the girls listened at the top of the stairs and he said everyone was sounding quite merry. We had two or three gallon jugs of wine among us and I don't think anyone was feeling any pain. Betty was also an English war bride. She took a writing course from a very well known Canadian writer and her daughter married his son.

That spring while trying on my summer dresses I realized that I was getting a little chubby, maybe tucking in a little too well over the winter, but sometimes I felt rather nauseous in the mornings, and the doctor told me there would be a new little person coming soon. So most of that summer I waddled and lumbered around.

I was most happy when my waddling came to an end and Timothy Allan Dahm said hello to the world on November 13th of that year 1963, weighing exactly eight pounds, and measuring twenty inches. As with the other miniature Dahms, he was exactly the way babies are supposed to look, pink and white, and gold, with very blue eyes.

He was such a considerate baby, sleeping through the night, very early in his little life. We all liked waking him up because he was always so happy, just beaming at everyone. He was also a very strong baby and very curious. Relatives, friends and neighbours, all came to see the new baby and agreed what a happy little chap he was.

Ours was a busy household, for it was thirteen years since there was a baby in the Dahm household and the days seemed very full. In less than a year Timmie was walking, terribly pleased with himself and getting into everything he shouldn't and as he got a little older, we had to keep a very watchful eye on him when he was playing outside.

One wintery weekday morning early the next spring, Allan was at work and the girls were at school, Timmie was playing outside. He was supposed to stay in view of the windows, and he usually did, but this time I couldn't see him. My first thought was the river. I scrambled down the bank and then I saw him making his way down the river. He was within shouting distance so I called out to him, "Don't move, stay right there."

This was springtime when ice gets very thin. When I caught up with him I told him over and over and over, that he must never go to the river again, that the river could be a very dangerous place, he must never go there alone, only when Mummie or Daddie were with him, or Terrie and Janine. Thankfully he never did. This was one of the scariest moments he gave us, and it all happened in seconds. He was never outside alone more than a few minutes, always where I could see him. It was quite some time before

I let him play outside alone again. I would always go with him.

As there were no small children nearby, Allan and I thought it might be a good idea to send him to nursery school or pre-school. I took him along to several schools, asked about their programmes and the hours. I suppose I checked out about six nursery schools altogether.

Timmie at his first school, The Cat in the Hat.

We settled on one called, *The Cat in the Hat.* This was run by a Mrs. Ott, a very likable person and she appeared to genuinely like children, and Timmie seemed to like her. So it was decided that she would pick him up on the following Monday. But when Mrs. Ott came for him, he was quite reluctant to go. I told him that Mrs. Ott would bring him back home again. I said, "You will come back, it won't be very long, you will meet new friends, and you will have fun." He whimpered a little. Mrs. Ott and I didn't know quite what to do, so I said maybe we will try it this once, and if he is unhappy, we won't continue. After all, he was only a little over three, just a baby.

He was gone a little over two hours. The first thing he told me on his return was, "There, I told you I would come back," repeating what I had told him. And Mrs. Ott didn't have to tell me that he liked his new experience for his excited chatter recounting his time away told me it all. One of his favourite make-believe things was playing kindergarten, but I could never be Mrs. Ott, Timmie always had to be Mrs. Ott, and I had to be Timmie. His time spent in kindergarten was a wonderful learning experience. After a little snack in the afternoon it would be 'lesson time'. He would tell me the names of numbers, letters and colours, and the names of pictures, then he would draw me a little picture, I'd read him a little story before he had a little nap.

Allan, Timmie and me at Timmie's university graduation.

1966, the year of Terrie's graduation. She made her own graduation dress and she did look so pretty when Jim Duffin called for her. He had borrowed his dad's car for the occasion. Theirs was a rather stormy relationship and it didn't last. Jim had quite a fiery temper and would get rather jealous. Terrie had a mind of her own and she didn't want to be controlled. It was inevitable that their dating would end. We heard many years later Jim became a lay preacher and I'm sure he grew into a very nice man.

Janine was almost sixteen, and she too was going out on dates. I don't know if the teen years and early twenties are more confusing for girls or boys. Certainly a difficult time, when one is trying to find out who they are, and what they would like to do with their lives. Even so, I'm sure both Terrie and Janine had a lot of happy times in those years.

It appears that the word 'teenager' was coined after the Second World War. There always have been teenagers and there always will be, but before the Second World War, they were not considered to be 'a separate society'. It seemed to me, that *we*, their parent generation, had to mature a lot sooner than they do nowadays. From observation I would say as a general rule, it gets easier economically for every subsequent generation of teenagers. Of course, this doesn't hold true in every case and it might not be psychologically easier for them in today's world.

Both the girls worked for the City of Calgary Recreation Department planning programmes of activities for groups of children and I must say they did very well at this job. I'm happy to say both Terrie and Janine were talented in arts and crafts.

Terrie designed a poster for the Cancer Society that was used in one of their campaigns and she could make clothing that looked as if it came directly from London or Paris couturiers; and Janine working with children and others and created many novel activities.

In her high school years Janine used to arrive at school very early to take part in gym activities and she was fond of Physical Education. She loved to ride. She was quite happy when she could borrow Louella's' horse *Chiato*. Terrie did a little bit of riding, but she was not nearly as keen for it as Janine was. By this time the girls no longer took part in Louella's little shows, they had too many other pursuits.

When Terrie completed the poster for the Cancer Society, there was a dinner put on at the *Highlander Hotel*, for students and their parents who made valued contributions. They served prime rib of beef and Yorkshire pudding with roast potatoes and a vegetable medley, also salad, and apple pie for dessert, a very good meal.

We were seated at a table with another couple and their daughter, who were very terribly retiring. It was rather sad, we tried to make them feel more relaxed, but I think they would all rather have been in Timbuktu than sitting at a table with three strangers in the *Highlander*, and none of them liked prime rib either. The lady quietly asked Allan if he would like to have some of her beef, and Allan did take some, but it is not something you can comfortably do with strangers.

Everyone got through the evening, which was rather a stiff affair, as most such functions are wont to be, and I'm sure most present were glad when the evening came to an end. However, everyone was proud of the achievements of the children, especially their own.

Janine and Terrie both worked that summer, but Janine would have to go back to school. Terrie's first full time job was at the *Royalite Service Station* on Sixteenth Avenue in Montgomery, where she worked in the coffee shop. Not the most pleasant of jobs, for not all the customers were well mannered. She didn't stay there very long because she definitely did not want to make a lifetime career of it, but it was just one more learning experience in the book of life.

The girls learned one or two things about neighbours when they were asked to babysit. One neighbour who called himself a friend even asked for a nickel change, stating that he didn't have the correct amount. Even at their youthful age, the girls surmised he was a very tight, penny-pinching, individual.

There was one family where Terrie stayed babysitting

for about a week. This woman simply wouldn't pay Terrie. We phoned two or three times, and I wrote a letter to her asking, "Will you please pay my daughter the amount you owe her for babysitting for you?" She just ignored our pleas. And it was only when Allan, who was then Deputy Clerk of the Court in Calgary wrote a letter to her with a return address, Deputy Clerk of the Court, did she respond. Very quickly too, for an envelope found its way into our mailbox with a cheque inside, and I suspect it was put there under cover of darkness. This was very shabby treatment, since Terrie had taken food from home, as there wasn't enough food in the house for the children. And one or two of the beds were in need of sheets, so we sent those along too.

Then there was the house they called, *Borderline*. It seems to me both girls took turns staying with the children there. Another example of not enough food for the children and a baby in a soaking wet crib. You have no choice but to help in such a situation, and so we did. I think getting paid for that experience was also like pulling teeth. The girls gradually learned that not everyone in this world is honest.

Somewhere along the way, Terrie took a course in Chinese painting and did quite well, but she didn't need any lessons in sewing or dressmaking. Sewing came naturally to her. She certainly didn't inherit the talent from me, though I did make quite a few things for the girls when they were quite small, and for their dollies as well. Janine took a sewing and dressmaking course and did make a few things, but it wasn't her best endeavour.

1966 - Timmie's fourth Christmas. His first Christmas he was oblivious to, being just a few weeks old. He was filled with wonder at the Christmas tree and its decorations, on his second Christmas, touching the ornaments very gingerly and saying, "ooh, ooh." But this Christmas that little man knew a lot more about the old elf in the red suit, and he wanted to be in there helping with preparations and decorations. I wondered if that Christmas outfit from last year would fit him if I made a few adjustments? Christmas gave way to Boxing Day and then New Year's Eve. All happy times with the family and friends. Looking back over those crowded times, I wonder how we managed to do it, but we did, and there were always many willing hands ready to help.

Terrie would be nineteen that year, and Janine seventeen. Maybe the reader is wondering how our family escaped the terrible teen years of the sixties? Well, we didn't.

City Lights
by *Muff-Anne York-Hayley*

(from her book: *Even October Has Something to Say*)

City lights
Seducing me
With their pulsating pulchritude,
Sepulchrally beseeching me
To stay,
For just one more night
And one more day.

The distance between myself and this city,
At times becomes
A void
Too wide
To comprehend.

The crowds, the noise,
The smells, the aloneness,
Have entrapped
My mind
In an invisible vise
City life.

The girls led us a merry old dance during that time being involved with the hippies, the communes, and the flower-child movement. It was a time when they considered their parents were terribly *'square'* and should be hidden away, unacknowledged. And to say they didn't like us very much, is putting it mildly, and I must say in all honesty that the feeling was quite mutual. Fortunately for everyone that situation didn't last forever. Everybody we knew that had teenagers went through the same exasperating experience.

It was the year Terrie worked as a go-go dancer in one of the nightclubs in Calgary, and later that year; she went to Toronto with one of the girls from the commune where she lived. Even though the relationship between us was strained, we did miss her when she left. But we were glad that some of the stress and tension was lifted from our lives.

But there was still Janine who certainly had a mind of her own, quite sure that the main purpose of parents was to be wet blankets and fun spoilers, and certainly they didn't understand anyone or anything!

I could have told them, and maybe I should have told them about my experience working as a hostess in a ·nightclub in London. It was in the war years and some of the patrons mistakenly took me for a 'lady of the evening', for why else would I be working there. Needless to say, my time there was quite short.

Terrie went to Woodstock while living in Eastern Canada. She heard Gordie Lightfoot and Janis Joplin, and brought back many good memories with her. But I don't think her sojourn there was all that she had hoped it would be. She arrived back in Calgary on her birthday in October of that year and I remember Gram very quickly making a little birthday cake for her. That was most thoughtful. Gram was staying with us, as she did on many weekends and special occasions, birthdays, Mothers Day, Thanksgiving, Christmas and Easter.

Wigs were in fashion at that time and Terrie was wearing a short curly wig that looked very good on her. I remember Timmie taking it and putting it on and he looked like a cute little lion. It was a pleasant occasion and we were all glad to see one another again.

The end of October, where did that year go, I couldn't believe that it was almost gone. My clothes once again were bursting at the seams. I hoped that my clothes would fit me better around the end of March – and they did.

1968 and Timmie got himself a little brother on March 31st, Christopher Robin. He weighed in at seven pounds, a pound lighter than Timmie. He was born with a broken collarbone, a headache and a stretched neck, but the doctor said there was nothing wrong with his waterworks as he had wee'd all over him. They kept him in an isolette for a while 'til he got stronger. He was rather a sad little chap, all ragged and broken.

He didn't have the happiest babyhood for he was not very well and he was allergic to milk. His formula was made with Soylac. Even when he was on solid foods, the only thing he really liked was Flings, which was a treat made from puffed corn. Timmie said he was his weak baby and he was going to call him *Boo-Boo*. I think he quite liked having a baby brother.

Timmie and Christopher.

Timmie and Christopher with the Easter Bunny.

Timmie was now four and half, and when Allan was working around the house or outside, Timmie was right behind him wanting to know the purpose of every tool and what Daddie was going to do next. And he saved Daddie a lot of steps fetching things from the house or the shed. When you have an acreage it was always a long way back to the house to fetch something you may have forgotten.

Timmie was very good at amusing himself. He would play alone for long periods but whenever he could, he loved to help Daddie. And Allan spent a lot of time playing with him before bedtime. Christopher wasn't big enough to play yet, but whenever he couldn't sleep, we'd take him for a car ride and it worked like magic.

At one point we had a very anxious time with Timmie. The doctor put him in the hospital for several tests as his white blood count was very high, and Leukemia was suspected. How relieved and happy we all were when this was not the case. The high white blood count was due to a bad infection. We sure did miss his cheery little presence around the house and he seemed very glad when he came back to his own little room again.

We found it necessary to plan a small wedding for Janine and her boyfriend, Norman. Janine was due to have a baby the following May. This was sprung on us quite suddenly, Christmas was almost upon us, but thought we would make it the nicest little wedding we could at such short notice. This didn't suit Norman's parents, who wanted a large affair, with about two hundred guests. The affair we had planned was to be in the new family room, for about thirty people.

I couldn't tell whether these were Janine's wishes as well, or just those of Norman's parents, or maybe she was just easily led. As the whole thing was taken away from us we didn't attend the wedding, and certainly the way they handled the wedding was a breach of etiquette. It could be they were not aware of this fact, but it's senseless to stay upset about these things forever.

Looking at the pictures from the wedding, I must say Janine made a very lovely bride. I remember very well what we did that day. Terrie was staying with us for a little while, and to take our minds off unhappy circumstances, we took the boys and Terrie and went to the zoo. It was a grey day that November 30th, 1968, and it was quite nippy. Kay and Walter, Allan's aunt and uncle, attended the wedding, and later that evening they dropped in for a visit.

Sometime before this Terrie had met Jordan, a musician who sang and played guitar with a group called, *The Family Portrait*, and you could say that was a serious affair, so we were not traumatized when Terrie became pregnant. However, Terrie and Jordan had stopped seeing one another before the baby was born. Shortly after Janine's wedding, in the early part of December, Allan took Terrie to the Foothills Hospital where she gave birth to a little girl. It was a very hard decision to make, as I am sure it must be for all girls in similar situations, but Terrie put the baby up for adoption. Allan and I had talked about adopting the baby, but on reflection, realized it would not be fair or wise. Many years later, Terrie and her daughter were to look for one another and eventually found each other.

That was Christopher's first Christmas, but at nine months he wasn't too interested in celebrations and preparations. Relatives and friends said nice things about him as people are wont to do about babies and this pleased his parents. I remember our family doctor, who attended Terrie in the hospital, popped in for a little visit that year.

May 21st, 1969 - Janine came with me to visit Timmie's kindergarten. Half way through the morning I had to phone Allan to tell him it was time to take Janine to the hospital. He arrived in a big blue Ford truck that we called, *Brutus* to escort Janine to the Foothills maternity ward where she had a little boy, Patrick Blain, born on his father's birthday. Poor Allan was so embarrassed. For the third time in just over a year he made this trip taking women to the maternity ward at the Foothills Hospital. He was quite sure the nurses were giving him very strange looks and thinking he was not a very nice man. I tried to reassure him, telling him there were probably different nurses on duty each time he made those trips. But he wouldn't be convinced. *Brutus* had now become dubbed the *baby buggy*.

Summer time again, time for gardens and flowers, barbecues and campfires, relatives and friends. Timmie was registered in St. Bernard's School starting grade one in September and I think he was looking forward to it. He had an enquiring mind and seemed to enjoy learning new things. I drove him there, as I had my driver's license by then.

Terrie took up her friendship with Jordan again. I wondered if he ever saw the baby, or if his parents did. She was a nice little baby, not fair as all the Dahms seemed to be. She had a lot of dark hair like Jordan and her eyes were very blue. I hoped that she had gone to a good home.

I truly don't remember why we put in such a large garden. We seemed to only use about a tenth of it, all the rest was given away. Beside, I've always favoured flowers over vegetables.

135

Some years ago we had had some landscaping done. Poor Chester, the landscaper, was rather a sad man. I'm sure he meant well, but he didn't have any idea about landscaping, and I really did feel sorry for him, after all, he was just trying to earn a living. He had grandiose ideas in his head but he couldn't carry them out in reality.

Allan built the dearest little pump house that year to protect the well pump from the elements. Sometimes he would have to spend hours in there when the pump had lost its prime simply because some mischief-makers thought what tremendous fun it would be to take the line out of the river giving the home owner no end of trouble. On one of these occasions Allan swore if he found the culprits responsible he would kick their bloody arses over the moon. Upon hearing this, Bertha, our Dutch friend commented, "Ja, if it is impossible you can do it!"

I am probably getting repetitive and boring when I say that Thirteenth Avenue on the river was a wonderful place to live and a wonderful place to bring up children. However, many river ramblers thought our property was public parkland and came scrambling up the bank through our property. One incident stays in my mind, of one poor woman making her way up the bank with a swarm of hornets following her. I sprayed her with insect repellent, put iodine on a couple of stings she had, gave her a cold drink, and had her rest a while.

That was the year that the *Calgary Herald* reporter came to the house to take the picture of the five generations. There was Allan's grandmother, Allan's mother, Allan, Janine, and Patrick Blain, straight blood line. We made the occasion cause for celebration and had a very happy social evening.

Also the year that a picture of the Dahm scarecrow made it to the *Calgary Herald* "complaining that he was very tired and needed a rest," so said the caption. It was probably October.

By this time, Christopher was able to toddle around and explore the property that was his home, and Timmie was telling us of his adventures in his new school.

Chapter 10

More River Bank

We had experienced many changes in Shouldice Park since moving there seventeen years previously in 1952. The park now had a swimming pool and a clubhouse, a well-appointed recreation hall, as well as ball diamonds. There was an inside skating rink, and they had added picnic tables and outside hibachis. We could enjoy a swim and a picnic just by walking a few yards from home.

I remember a swimming hole down by the trailer court where the local kids would cool off on hot days. That trailer court, I never knew how it came to be. It seemed to just spring up overnight, like a mushroom. I know it wasn't always there and Thirteenth Avenue wasn't always Thirteenth Avenue.

Thirteenth Avenue when we first moved there in 1952 was called Bow Avenue which brings to mind Bow, a fat little puppie that waddled up from the river one day, so the obvious name for him was Bow. We would have loved to keep him but had to give him up when a sad little boy came looking for his lost puppie.

Tales of the river bank wouldn't be complete without telling of the *Helen and Fred Episode,* our old friends from Deer Lodge. They were living in a trailer but had no place to put it. So we told them just bring it along and park it on the property. Certain neighbours, however, took a rather un-Christian attitude to this and phoned the city hall saying their trailer was an eyesore. This, when we were surrounded by wild prairie, was quite ludicrous. This was before all the improvements took place in Shouldice Park. But Helen and Fred did stay quite a while. Nothing more was said about Helen and Fred's trailer after this. I think the city was rather glad of the revenue that Tourism brought.

There were a few enterprising neighbours who thought they would make hay while the sun shone and would make money while the Calgary Stampede was in progress, putting signs on their properties saying trailer parking and camping. This distressed some of the neighbours on Thirteenth Avenue and there seemed to be rivalry between the *campsite owners* who would take one another's signs down and hide them. They had a merry old time with their word battles and sign snitching, but I don't think the situation ever came to fisticuffs!

Stampede time brings to mind one of our fair weather friends who came to visit us at that time with his wife and two little boys. He was once our neighbour. I don't know if they had looked, but they said they couldn't find accommodation anywhere because the city was so full of Stampede visitors. So we told them they could stay in the little place, the former chicken house. We had left it furnished and it was quite self-contained, with a bathroom and we always kept non-perishable foods in the cupboards. It even had the *luxury* of a fridge! It would accommodate the four of them very well. We often used the little place on weekends just for fun, to make a little change. Of course, they were delighted to find this private motel at zero rates and they stayed for the duration of the Stampede and then they left. We neither saw nor heard from them ever again.

The last day of 1969 and we were as usual getting ready for quite a few relatives and friends who would welcome 1970 in with us. We had planned to wake Timmie and let him stay up for a little while and sing *Auld Lang Syne*, but we agreed that Christopher would much rather have slept as it didn't mean much to one so young.

Early that January Terrie asked Harvey if he would drive her to Edmonton where she was going to live with Jordan who was working there. Of course, dear old Harvey could never say no to anyone. He did ask her though, "Have you told your folks, and if you haven't, then I must tell them, because they will be worried about you."

We kept in touch with Terrie but she didn't stay in Edmonton very long. She wrote to say that she and Jordan would like to get married and that they'd like to get married at home. They came down in early May. Terrie stayed with us at home, and Jordan stayed with his parents.

Jordan had taken some instruction in Catholic doctrine, so he knew a little about the Catholic faith. We had been busy some time before this meeting with Father Gerharz, going over the plans for the Mass and the music they would like played. We spent a lot of time going over reception plans with Terrie and Jordan, and his parents; what kind of reception, how many guests, what kind of food would they would like served. There were the invitations to send out, the rehearsal, and many other little details that had to be attended to.

The date was set for May 17th, my sister's birthday. Sadly though, she couldn't attend because she was in England. There were probably between thirty-five or forty of us at the wedding, including the bride and groom, Jordan's parents, and Allan and I, an intimate affair. I would be very remiss if I didn't mention the wonderful job Janine did with the flowers. Previously she had worked for some time at *Ted Brooks Florists* in Calgary and knew all about flower arranging. She put many hours in doing such a good job for her sister's wedding.

One of Jordan's relatives at the wedding who worked at one of the Calgary television stations stated that she hoped she could do as well when planning her daughter's wedding. We were most pleased.

With Allan, Janine, and Harvey helping, we were all very happy with the way it turned out. Harvey and I made the wedding cake together, but it was Harvey who made it into a work of art when he decorated it.

We loaned the couple our car to go to Banff, where they went for their honeymoon. We must have by that time owned that lemon of a gas gobbler the International Travel-all, for I know *we* weren't left without transportation ourselves.

When they came back from Banff they told us over and over they thought their wedding was perfect in every detail. Knowing they were happy with it, was all that was needed to make it worthwhile. They thought Timmie made a dear little ring-bearer, taking his part quite seriously, and wasn't it nice that they each had a sister who were the bridal attendants, and Jordan had a brother who was the best man. They went back to live in Edmonton for a while, where Jordan was still working.

1971 – Christopher turned three at the end of March, and on July 27th, we had been married twenty-five years. We planned a celebration for quite a few people, hoping that the weather would be kind to us, so that it could take place outside.

So, once again, we sent invitations and I wondered how we might let people know that we did not want gifts. I asked Harvey, who was helping write the invitations, how we might do this without being presumptive. Harvey quipped, "Just write, gifts gratefully accepted at the back door."

"Oh be serious Harvey," I told him, "it is rather a delicate subject, we just want people to come and celebrate with us, we don't want any 'stuff', we have quite enough 'stuff'."

And who helped make the cake, none other but Harvey. We had a lot of fun making that cake; so many odds and ends went into it but it did turn out quite well. We threw in broken cookies, hard cake, fruit salad, peaches that needed using up, some jam in the bottom of a jar, marmalade, and, oh yes, yogurt. At one point Harvey thought he'd found something else to put in it. "Oh," I said, "not that, it's dog food." When Harvey finished decorating the cake, it looked much too good to eat, but we did eat it, and all of it.

Al Gow, a Court House friend, tended bar for us, which gave Allan a break, and he was able to visit more. We had a lady who came in, who often helped us in the house. She came on that day with her daughters and took care of most of the serving.

We had cooked a ham, a turkey, and a baron of beef, with side dishes of buns and salads and relishes, stuff like that. I think Gram must have done the carving, for she did it so well, and it wasn't Allan's favourite activity. The party really went off very well.

The company was good. All in all, there must have been upwards of one hundred and fifty came that day, and we were very glad that the weather was very kind to us and that we could enjoy the outdoors. And there were many, many gifts, even though we had said, 'please no gifts'. The Court House staff had collected over three hundred silver dollars and Art Godfrey, a Court House friend, had painted a special wooden chest silver, and put all the silver dollars in there, putting two little keys in a pink envelope and two little keys in a blue envelope, a most thoughtful thing to do. Gordon, the Sheriff, made the presentation to us and we were surprised indeed.

In the evening we lighted a fire in the fire pit. Regulations concerning backyard fires were not nearly as stringent in those years. We had coloured lanterns hanging from the trees. Tony Waloshyn, another Court House friend, had brought his music along. Some couples were dancing, and others were just enjoying the music and the fire, and where music is played, there are some that are absolutely compelled to sing.

Later that evening some of the guests were wondering if there were any hot dogs. The Dahm's freezer always had the makings of hot dog treats, as we had many backyard fires, and took many weekend trips to Bragg Creek and to Okotoks where we cooked hot dogs and marshmallows. The last of our guests left around three in the morning, very tired, but very happy, and as *we* were *also* very tired, we left the mess and said, "Let's think about it tomorrow." After a good sleep we started in with a feverish energy, but it happened, as it did on many of these occasions, there were always willing hands coming to help us clean up, which always turned into a social time and the work never got finished. But we did make a start!

And while we were trying to make order out of the chaos, Timmie decided he would try out the electric hedge trimmer and nearly took the top of his finger off. He had had so many warnings to leave all the power tools strictly

141

alone, but Timmie was always so curious about everything. He was rather quiet for a while after this. Maybe he was planning what his next adventure would be, or was he thinking he was a lucky little boy to have such a narrow escape from a bad accident.

We were still with the *Hypnosis Society* and they made Allan and I joint president, probably because no one else wanted the job. I touched on our square dancing spree with *The Melody Squares* of Montgomery and told you of our time with the Scottish country dancers, but I don't think I've touched on the fun we had when we took up Latin dancing. I don't remember the name of the instructor, but I do remember he made it a fun time and most of us could do a rumba, samba, tango, or any Latin dance that was popular at that time without too much trouble. When Harvey was visiting here in Vernon last year, he asked me if I remembered 'single-single, double-double', a phrase the instructor chap used to make the step stay with us.

It was around this time I took the course, *Owner, Know Your Car.* Of course I knew my car. It had four wheels to run on and it had a steering wheel to turn it and you had to put fuel in it. It had to have the right number of spark plugs and needed oil to run smoothly and it had something called a distributor. Other than this, I knew very little, so I thought I must need to take the course. I think I learned something from it, at least I hope I did, for I'm not very mechanically minded. During the course, I met Albert, who was from Bombay. He was a draughtsman with an engineering firm in Calgary and he had been in Canada for some years. The course went for three hours once a week, I don't remember how many weeks.

As the course was quite long for an evening course, we had a little break, and little chatters with the other students. During one of these breaks, Albert asked me, "Do you have a dog?"

"Yes, I have a dog, his name is Tommie," I told him.

He wanted to know if I had a husband and family. "I have a husband," I said, "and we have two grown daughters, and two little boys."

"But you don't wear a ring," he said.

"I haven't for many years, arthritis has made my hands quite gibbled, making it impossible to wear rings," I explained.

Albert said he felt that my husband must be a very fine fellow and he would like to meet him and my family. So it was arranged that he would come for dinner and I made a curry. I guess it reminded him of home and I suppose he was glad to have someone cook for him for a change for he was a bachelor. We did become quite friendly.

There was a chap taking the course who came from Pakistan and I did get more than a little cross with him because he told me that he didn't like Canada and that when he made enough money, he was going back to his own country. I told him that I liked Canada. "Canada has been very good to me," I said. I don't think that I would have enjoyed such a good lifestyle if I had remained in England, though sometimes I do get overwhelmed with nostalgia.

I remember one very nice lady taking the *Owner, Know Your Car* course. We talked about the wisdom, or the lack of it when picking people up who were hitchhiking. That very evening I had given an off duty policeman a ride to the station, and he told me that I should never pick anyone up, but he was glad that I had given him a ride. The lady I was talking to, was a good sized lady and said, "All I'd have to do is sit on them if they gave me any trouble. You're too small, you couldn't defend yourself." At the end of the course, this same lady brought a tray of wonderful home baked goodies for the entire class to enjoy.

I didn't see any of the group again, except Albert did visit. Although he owned a car, a Ford Galaxy, he told us he did not have his license. I offered to take him to get his license. It took him a couple of tries, but he did get it and he was quite delighted.

Albert was going back to India to choose a bride. It seems she had to have a sponsor in Canada and Albert asked Allan if he would sponsor her. He agreed to do this for Albert.

When he came back to Canada, his mother and his

bride-to-be, Shirley, and her sister came with him. We invited them all for a social evening. In the course of the evening when his mother was outside looking at the garden, he told us that he had chosen another girl, but she didn't meet with his mother's approval. Whether she must have had the father's approval also, I'm not sure.

As we got to know Shirley better we liked her very much. She was a most worthwhile person and in Bombay she had been a kindergarten teacher. We found Albert's mother, and Shirley's sister, Angela, quite delightful.

Albert's brother Clarence, whom we called Clarry, came to Canada not too long after he did. He came to the house a few times with an Irish girl, Mary, who was a nanny.

One weekend Albert came to visit when I was about to plant a little Nanking Cherry and Albert said he would do that for me. Poor Albert, he no sooner dug the spade in than he complained of exhaustion. He thought he might be having heart problems. Albert was not used to physical labour. In Bombay they had seven or eight servants to do everything for his family.

Shirley and Albert were married in the Sacred Heart Church in Calgary by Father Stevenson. It was a very nice affair with quite a few guests. Later, Shirley's sister came to Canada a couple of times on her own again, and then she came with her parents. It must have been for the christening of Shirley and Albert's first little girl, Arleen. They came for an evening, but sadly we only saw them once. We would have liked to have seen more of them and of Albert's mother.

Allan and I and Harvey took a ballroom dance course in the fall. We always had fun at these things. Harvey usually came for dinner on that night and sometimes after the course we went for a glass of beer and a little socializing with others from the dance group.

All was not going well with Janine and Norman. She left him for a while and came to live in the little house with Paddie. I guess they must have smoothed things over because before too long Norman moved in with them.

We made a stab at cross-country skiing and quite enjoyed it. Janine and Paddie always came with us, sometimes Bertha and Leo. On one occasion, coming down the incline at the top of our property with Bertha, I slipped and fell. Rolling in the snow with my skis waving in the air, flapping around like a fish out of water. "Here, take my pole," said Bertha, "don't make me laugh, I pee the pants."

Times spent with Bertha and Leo were always pleasant. Each had a wonderful sense of humour. Leo had built the large family room onto the back of the house and the conservatory on the river side. There were other projects besides. Bertha and Leo were both from Holland. Like so many new Canadians from Europe in those days, their memories were crowded with not such happy times during the Nazi Occupation of their countries.

The Nazis had forcefully taken over Leo and Bertha's Netherlands farm. One morning, while they were having breakfast in the kitchen, the officer in charge of the confiscation, burst into the room shouted orders, stormed out again and left the door open. Leo kicked it shut. The officer came raging back again and said, "If your wife weren't pregnant, I would shoot you," then added insult to injury when he kicked Leo's backside.

Sara, another Court House friend, used to get quite low on weekends so I suggested that Allan ask her to come cross-country skiing with us. She came quite a few times. I usually made a big pot of chili and she stayed for dinner and we watched a bit of TV together. Sometimes we played pool. Once her boyfriend came with her. "Come skiing with us," she said.

"No, no my back, you know about my bad back."

After when we were playing pool, she tried to get him to play.

"No, no, I don't think so, my back, bad back you know."

"Gee, you're a dull turd," she said. Maybe he was, he could have been, but rather a nice one.

It was around this time I began to experience a lot of distress in the lower abdomen. I knew things didn't feel quite right, but some days I would be almost free from distress, so I didn't see any need to go to the doctor. But when the discomfort persisted, I thought I should see what it was all about.

The doctor ordered various tests that were standard procedure for such miseries. There were x-rays, some kind of scope that begins with an "s" and I can't even say it. Then there were barium enemas, and other enemas, ugly things. I don't think these are given any more; things are much more sophisticated now. During that time of tests I didn't have a shred of dignity left. The outcome of all the prodding and probing showed I had an intestinal infection. They kept me in hospital for a few days then let me go home.

This didn't clear up the problem and I was in and out of the hospital while they tried to determine the real problem. I was told they would have to do a hysterectomy. I suppose I had to agree with their prognosis, but when I came out of the anaesthetic, the nurse informed me that they didn't have to perform the hysterectomy after all.

Later the doctor told me that part of the intestine was diseased and it would have to be removed, but this would not be done right away. I would have to have a colostomy. At the thought of this, I told him I would rather die. He said that would certainly happen any way if the poisons weren't eliminated from my system. He then told me to think it over and give him my answer the next morning.

Who would take care of Timmie and Christopher? Who would take care of Allan? It wouldn't be fair to leave them all alone. I wasn't being noble, but I just didn't think I was ready to die yet, my work down here wasn't finished. I asked the doctor to let me out for the weekend because I wanted to take Timmie and Christopher on an outing, not knowing how long this whole procedure would take or how I would handle it.

I was kept in hospital for some time after the colostomy. Doctors, nurses and counsellors tried to help with the psychological effects and someone from the Ostomy Society came to talk to me along with other Ostermates, as we were called. Everyone saying it was quite possible to lead a normal life, when all the while I was feeling absolutely shattered and embarrassed.

After being discharged from the hospital I wouldn't answer the door, I didn't want to see anyone. People left flowers outside the door. After a month of this self-pity, I became absolutely weary of myself and decided to make the best of the situation. I was a lot luckier than most people with colostomies as I would only have it for several months. It was a transverse colostomy and not permanent.

It was time to get on with the business of living. I joined a drama group and told them right at the beginning that if they heard any strange noises such as motorbikes starting up, not to look at one another, it would be me, for I had a colostomy. We had fun in that drama course; we performed *Crawling Arnold* by Jules Pfeifer. I played Grace Enterprise. We put it on at Paget Hall in Calgary to a sold out house.

1972 - Janine was still living in the little house with Paddie. Norman lived there with them for a little while, but sadly, that relationship was doomed from the start. Janine was still working at *Ted Brook's* the florist where she did very well learning the art of flower arranging. Allan was the chauffeur, he would drop Paddie off at Mrs. Koernig's the babysitter, a very kindly woman, then drop Janine off at *Ted Brook's* and proceed downtown to the Court House. Reversing the procedure, Janine would come home with Allan picking up Paddie at the babysitter's.

Christopher was four on the 31st of March, 1972 and Paddie was three on May 21st. Christopher and Paddie played together all the time, not always amicably though, for Paddie, though a year younger than Christopher, seemed quite determined to have his way, though Christopher wouldn't always let this happen.

As summer came around, of course veggie gardens and flowers began to occupy our time. We certainly missed those days of July and August when Allan first started to work at the Court House when they only worked half days. Those halcyon days seemed to go on forever. Nothing seemed the same when the staff began working full time through July and August.

This was the year that we contracted Leo to build the 24' x 24' family room onto the back of the house. French doors led onto a large landing with a couple of steps going down. The room had large windows and a very high ceiling. You could also enter through a side door leading onto a gallery and then down two or three steps into the room itself. Many people could be packed into that room and what good times we had there.

Don Oliver, Allan's best army friend, and his wife, May, spent a week with us at Stampede time. We had a fun time with them and I was glad to finally meet Don and May. That same year, their son Ralph, his wife and little boy, paid us a visit. They were a nice little family

Janine enrolled at Mount Royal College taking a course in recreational therapy. It was a three-year course focusing on how to help the mentally and physically handicapped, the visually impaired, and those others with special needs. She did well with the course, whilst taking care of Paddie at the same time. He was at our house quite a bit playing with Timmie and Christopher.

I think I might say without boasting, that all our children had their share of smarts, but Christopher was not academically inclined, but even at that young age, it was not hard to see he would eventually become an artist. The school years weren't pleasant ones for Christopher, and certainly weren't made any easier when weak points were commented on by his teachers in front of the class; quite the wrong approach. In later years he would tell us how he felt very embarrassed and it didn't do much for his self-esteem. Surely these methods belonged with the dunce cap, the strap and the cane.

Terrie was then managing a *Diet Centre* in Edmonton. She was awarded the golden or silver apple award for the work she did with the clients there. I'm not sure whether it was a golden apple or silver apple! She liked the work and the dieters seemed to experience good results from her work. She managed the *Diet Centre* for some time and eventually bought the business herself.

We enrolled Christopher in the kindergarten at St. Charles bilingual school in Calgary on the Crow Child Trail and Timmie, going on for ten years old was doing very well in school, earning very good marks.

1973 - Allan had a dream to build a large conservatory about 24′ x 24′ on the front of the house. It was to have floor to ceiling windows and a very high ceiling.

A recent sketch by son Christopher showing the large conservatory built onto the house in 1973.

We talked over our plans with Leo and it didn't take him long to start building it. It was a ten-sided building with ten long windows, above each window was a transom window. I don't know if I am giving these the correct name. All of the transom windows opened with the aid of a very long wooden pole, with two brass hook-like things on the end, which we had acquired. I know there must be a specific name for this pole, but I do not know it. It must have been at least a hundred years old.

There were steps leading from the front door down into the conservatory. When the building was completed we had gravel delivered that we ourselves spread on the floor. Then came the task of collecting slab rocks. This we did with the aid of Janine, Paddie, Harvey, and the boys, making it a fun time and afternoon picnic. Scouring places like Glenmore Dam and other sites where we knew rocks abounded.

We filled the conservatory with many plants. I phoned the Calgary Conservatory to ask if it would be wise to have budgies or canaries or finches flying around there. They advised against budgies and finches, but said that canaries would be okay, as they wouldn't destroy the plants, but my oh my, they sure did! They were certainly destructive little beggars but we were delighted to have them. I think at one time we must have had twenty or so canaries flying around that conservatory. The conservatory was a lovely place to have tea or lunch, or simply sit to watch and listen to the birds.

Twenty-one years before we had bought that property for the enormous sum of $2,500.00, at least that was how it seemed to us and at that time we wondered if we would ever be able to pay it off. The property saw many changes in the ensuing years. It became nicely landscaped, with a house of unusual design as the centerpiece. The little chicken house that we originally called home for five years had been renovated into a nice little guest house.

My involvement with the drama group continued and we staged *The Crucible* by Arthur Miller at Bowness High School. I played Judge Hawthorne, a most unlikely part for me because of my small size and my gender, but it was all in good fun, and we had quite a large audience attend.

Chapter 11

The Years Roll On

1974 - Things were unfolding as they should, I supposed. Christopher entered grade one that year and didn't like it any better than he liked kindergarten in St. Charles bilingual school. He never was a complainer, he just got on with the business at hand and made the best of it. We were quite pleased Timmie made the honour roll again. Janine was doing well at Mount Royal College with her courses and business was flourishing at the *Diet Centre* under Terrie's management and the clients were happy with their progress.

I took public speaking in the winter and it always seemed to be snowing a blizzard the night I went to the course. Harvey and I took a course in ceramics, and I'm quite sure he learned more than I did.

There was talk about the city expropriating some of our property to put a road through, but it never did come to pass. But there were developers interested in this choice property along the river. One developer told the area residents that his company had quite a few million dollars on hand and he was in a position to offer all the home owners on our strip of land along the river a very good price, but that did not come to pass either, and to the best of my knowledge, the property remains just as it was when we lived there over twenty years ago.

1975 - Janine finished her course in recreational therapy at Mount Royal College. We were there to see her receive her diploma. After the graduating exercises she came home and spent the rest of the day with us and the weather was kind. Janine already had a job lined up at *Providence Crèche* in Calgary. She did very well and the residents got on fine with her. Part of her job was planning

Christopher standing, a couple of pals and
Timmie at the monopoly board.

Allan mowing the place on Thirteenth Avenue.
The "borderline" house as we called it
in the background.

outings for them and recreational programmes, similar to her work in her summer holidays while still in high school, something that she really liked. She stayed at *Providence Crèche* three years gaining a lot of experience and then she was offered a job at the *CNIB* in Calgary. She found this work both challenging and rewarding while making friends with the people as she had done at *Providence Crèche*.

Time seemed to be moving along swiftly for all of us. The boys were growing up fast. Timmie was coming up twelve; Christopher was past eight, and Paddie over seven. When they weren't busy with their school work, they spent their time as young boys will, acting out the roles of fictional heroes such as Superman, Batman and Spiderman, and other legendary heroes, as Buffalo Bill and Wild Bill Hickcock. There was the game that Christopher and Paddie made up - they were Ace Men. I really didn't know what it was all about, but I do know this was a game that Timmie didn't like at all and he would tell them, "Stop, with your stupid Ace games." By and large they played together quite well without much discord, although Timmie liked to be the boss. Christopher and Paddie had taken an interest in art long before this time.

I can't remember exactly when visiting shut-ins became an interest for me. It may have started with Auntie Agnes, a widowed sister of Grampa, and Grace, a widowed cousin of Gram's. I became involved with the nursing homes and a Mrs. Davis who lived across from the *Bow View Nursing Home*; I may have met Mrs. Davis at the nursing home. I do remember though that our girls went to the Bow View a few times to entertain them with their dancing and singing.

Some of the nursing home ladies knitted squares, including Auntie Agnes and Mrs. Davis. Though I was never a 'craft' person, I did manage to produce 'squares'. Allan was very good at going round to the various stores in Calgary and begging for wool to help make these blankets. He would simply tell the storekeepers that we needed wool to make afghans for Oxfam, and I don't think he was ever refused. Allan also saved all of the Court House stamps for

Oxfam but I was not quite sure what they did with them. I think at one point we all collected used greeting cards for Oxfam and didn't know what they did with those either.

My children loved to make their own greeting cards and Christmas tree decoration from used cards and wallpaper samples. They also made decorations from foil envelopes that once contained soup and drink mixes, often in the shape of lanterns to hang on the tree, or cones to hold raisins, peanuts and animal crackers. I suppose we thought that these items would be healthier for them than eating too much candy. I'm a little wiser these days, for there is a tremendous amount of sugar in raisins, and I don't suppose animal crackers were the healthiest snack either.

1977 - Terrie and Jordan's marriage ended but it was heartening to know that they were still friends. We were distressed to hear recently he has Multiple Sclerosis but is still able to work a little.

Another year when various developers again vied with one another to get their hands on the choice properties along the Bow River. They were truly in earnest this time, and yet it all came to nought. I rather think that it had to do with city by-laws or zoning, or something like that. We all had meetings with the developers in some of our houses listening to them paint very rosy pictures. I imagine everyone thought they were going to be instant millionaires.

Allan and I had ideas at that time to look at houses in so-called upscale districts such as; Varsity Acres, Varsity Estates, and so forth. One realtor we talked to said we might make a deal on a house we quite liked in the Market Mall area in Calgary if we put up our property and some cash besides, we could have that house. The house was fifty thousand dollars. Later we were to sell our property for much, much, more. We have never lived anywhere since that we loved as much as our property on Thirteenth Avenue in Calgary.

1979 - Allan had been at the Court House for thirty years and decided that he would like to retire, and did. They gave Allan a wonderful retirement party and combined it with an anniversary celebration, as we had been married thirty-three years. It truly was an occasion to remember. He was called back to the Court House many times to help out even after he retired. We began to realize that the only way Allan could truly retire was if we moved to another province. Friends had told us that Vernon, in the Okanagan Valley, in British Columbia, was a very nice place to retire.

Did I tell you about the wedding of Terrie, (or Muff-Anne as she's called now since changing her name) to Peter Haley? They were married at home on Thirteenth Avenue a week after Allan's retirement party on his birthday, August 3rd. It was a very small wedding. There may have been thirty or thirty-five people all included and went off very well and they seemed quite happy with it.

A friend of Peter's from Ontario came west to be his best man and Janine was Terrie's matron of honour. Peter's mother and an aunt, also Mary, a sister of Peter's, came from down east and they stayed in the little house. Another sister of Peter's, Bonnie, came with her husband and joined them in the little house later. For Muff-Anne and Peter another milestone reached in their life's journey.

And now, many years later with two grown up daughters, they are still making that journey together. The Haley family has six dogs, ranging from very large to very small, and one cat called Francis. Rosey, their Korean pig left this place some time ago.

We lost our little dog, Tommie - neighbour's dogs killed him. He was such a dear little chap and quite a favourite around the neighbourhood. I think people found his cheekiness endearing. We were so heartsick that his little life came to such a violent close.

The Nesting
by *Timothy Allan Dahm*

It wasn't easy or elegant, as my Mum and Dad began
Living in a chicken coop, and an old Model A sedan.
The years went by,
and the Love they shared produced two little girls
Hard work and love turned
the shack they shared, into a castle adorned with pearls.
Good times they shared together, the fledgling family of four
There were dogs, cats, rodents, and plenty to explore.
Before too long
with the money they saved, they built a brand new home
They dug the holes
and drove the nails, and spread the dark brown loam.
The River of Life
She smiled at the love and warmth they shared
The River, She whispered to my Dad,
"There's more, so be prepared."
And The River
babbled quietly, and silently slipped on by
The River of Time
flowed silently, the clouds passed by on high.
The girls they grew
to women, and left the house they made
They struck out on their own at first,
uncertain and afraid.
More time slipped by,
an Angel came and blessed Mum two times more
Two little boys,
with choo–choos and toys, my Mother she bore.
As a child I can remember, the special place they made
The beauty and wonder, the fantasy where we played.
A special place
they made for us, with space and love and trees
Secrets, Tedbows, and Mrs. Ott
and flowers on the breeze.

Chapter 12

Westward Again

We went to Vernon to look at houses and property there. We were hoping to find something similar to our place on Thirteenth Avenue in Calgary. A small acreage with river or lake frontage, but sadly, nothing came close to our expectations. We looked at some pretty nice houses with surroundings which left much to be desired, then again a few places we looked at, the properties were charming but the houses were quite appalling.

After viewing many houses and walking around many properties, we settled on a three thousand square foot home on two and a half acres. There were sixteen apple trees on the site. That's wonderful we thought, but not really, for everyone in the Okanagan Valley appeared to have apple trees on their property, but at that time we didn't know it. We tried to convince ourselves that we had chosen wisely, but we were really not quite sure. The purchase of this house hinged on the sale of our property back in Calgary.

I found it difficult to believe that we were going to leave the spot that had been our home for twenty-eight years. We vowed when we moved there that we were never going to leave. With heavy hearts we tended to all of the details that moving entails and we left our old home with much sadness.

The party the neighbours gave us didn't do very much to lift our spirits. It only seemed to underline and finalize the fact that we really were moving. When we originally moved to Thirteenth Avenue in Calgary it didn't take a very large vehicle to transport all of our belongings, but at the time of the move we needed a very large moving van indeed.

Our Calgary house didn't stay on the market for too

long. Quite a few people came to see it. A lawyer who was at Allan's retirement party, and his wife, were quite enchanted with the house and the property. The lawyer didn't think I would remember him. "Of course I do," I told him, "You are Michael," (he had told me his name at Allan's retirement party), "you used to sell men's trousers at Selfridges in London. You asked for a raise and got the sack."

Shortly after we moved away from Thirteenth Avenue, Janine and Paddie left with *Bird* heading for Cannington, Ontario, which was *Bird's* or Alan's home town.

Our first night in the new house in Vernon we had to take mattresses and blankets from the camper and slept on the floor in the living room because the moving van didn't come until the next morning. Even then they failed to bring everything, informing us they would bring the remainder of our belongings in a couple of days when they were moving another family to Vernon.

On that day, looking at what seemed like thousands of boxes and furniture in disarray, we wondered if we would live long enough to make some kind of order out of all the chaos and disarray. (I wonder if everyone experiences these same feelings. Maybe not, for I have a friend who says she loves moving. "How can you love moving," I said, "it takes forever to get sorted out and some things you never do find.") It must have taken us the best part of a year to establish some kind of order, and truly some things we never did find.

I wondered if Michael, the lawyer who bought our Calgary house, and his family had settled in and sorted out. They had told us that they had wonderful plans to make the big family room into a living room and the conservatory they would convert into the master bedroom. Those were the plans, but sadly, they didn't come to pass for they did not stay together.

Many friends and relatives came to visit, anxious to see where we had settled in British Columbia. Most were quite taken with the house and its surroundings, but we knew deep in our hearts for us there could never be the attachment we felt for Thirteenth Avenue in Calgary. Our place there was the only place we thought of as really being home.

We had barely made the move to Vernon and had been there about ten days - when we were flying to Ontario for Janine's wedding. She was to marry Alan Dobson, nicknamed *Bird* by his mother, 'cos at one point in his life he was rather like a tall, skinny, bird! The wedding was held in Alan's parent's garden. Janine and Alan had known one another for some time and seemed to get on well together. It was a pretty wedding, Janine wore a long summery dress with a wreath of flowers in her hair. Alan's identical twin Ian, and his brothers looked very smart in their wedding finery. And Muff-Anne as matron on honour completed the bridal party. The little town where Janine and Alan were married was settled by ancestors of Alan's father who came over from Scotland.

Back home in Vernon we found the neighbours on East Vernon Road very friendly and helpful. One neighbour, Ed, gave us peaches from a tree in his yard, the first time any of us had tasted peaches straight from a tree. He found Timmie a job in his lumber company. Timmie would wait outside for Ed to come by in his truck and take him to work.

Dollie, a little part beagle dog we adopted in Vernon, would always wait patiently with him, no matter what the weather, and when the truck came, Timmie would let her inside.

Dollie had arrived when we answered an ad in the newspaper asking for a home for a red setter. The address given us was located in a little town about twenty miles away. Hazel Tee, the one who placed the ad, a very kind soul who took in stray animals, abused animals, and animals that no one wanted, took care of them and tried to find homes for them. The red setter she called *Red* had been a guard dog and she suspected that it may have been abused. She told us when we took him that if he didn't fit in she would take him back again. Sadly he didn't - he was too vicious. We took him back and made the acquaintance of another of Hazel's dogs - a little part beagle named Blondie. Hazel could see straight-away that we had fallen for her, and so she gave her to us.

Dollie had five delightful puppies soon after she arrived and we were able to find good homes for all of them. Poor Dollie's life was shortened by a reckless truck driver who swerved to the side of the road where she was walking. He didn't even stop. In the short time that Dollie was with us, she had become a very special member of our family.

Our first year on East Vernon Road was taken up with painting fences, house painting and renovations. Leo, who had also moved to British Columbia, came from Blind Bay about forty miles away to help. He often stayed over a couple of days to save the long drive back and forth and once or twice Bertha came with him. There was quite a bit of visiting back and forth with the neighbours and time passed very quickly.

We enrolled Christopher at St. James Catholic School and Timmie at Charles Bloom Secondary School in Lumby, about twenty miles or so from Vernon. Timmie had bought himself a 1967 Mercury Cougar that was his pride and joy, so he was able to drive back and forth. A school bus serviced St. James School but St. James School was not for Christopher. I don't think he liked the idea of uniforms for one thing. We then enrolled him in Hillview School, much nearer home. Timmie continued to work full time 'til he started school then he helped Ed on weekends.

In the meantime Ed and his family had moved from next door and we now had new neighbours, Marianne, Norman, and Sonia, their little girl.

We thought we would like to get some steers to raise for meat, so we ordered four delivered to Marianne and Norman. We opened the gate between our properties, and decided whichever two steers came through the gate onto the Dahm's would be ours. Right away we gave our steers names, Starsky and Hutch, and we more or less made pets of them. Sadly, it was too traumatic for us when they went to market and we quickly learned that raising steers was not for us and that was our first and only experience with raising cattle. Sending them to market made us feel like traitors.

Then there was the Dahm's chicken caper. We went to Armstrong where they held a farmer's market every Thursday, and bought ten chickens. I supposed there was a rooster among them. We felt quite pleased with ourselves and our purchase, but when we brought them home, most of them seemed to be minus their tail feathers. We discovered these chickens were quite mean spirited for they seemed to delight in pulling one another's feathers out and they were not the brightest creatures in creation. Allan built them six nests, but they all wanted to pile on the one nest and they dirtied in the nest too.

We bought fifteen more chickens over a period of time, it was nice to have the fresh eggs, and the neighbours were very glad to have fresh laid eggs at a very reasonable price. However, I don't count chickens among my favourite birds.

Our neighbours weren't the only ones who liked fresh eggs. Little Dollie dog sure loved eggs. Sometimes the chickens would lay their eggs in the strangest places but Dollie would persevere 'til she found them. She would look so guilty if we caught her in the act of taking them, but we didn't have the heart to scold her, especially after she worked so hard to find them in the first place.

Another chore that took quite a bit of time that first year was harvesting the apples. We bought a special ladder for this purpose and an orchardist who lived nearby explained that fruit trees had to be sprayed two or three times a year, and as he was quite handy, we had him do the job. The trees on our property were of the Spartan variety to be picked in early October, or was it late October?

Several things we quickly learned about apples that we hadn't known before. They arrive in tremendous quantities - sixteen trees yield a tremendous amount of fruit, what to do with all these apples? As it was our first year in Vernon, we hadn't met that many people, so we couldn't give many away. We gave some to a few charities, but we still had far too many left to eat ourselves, so what to do with the rest? People indicated that the supermarkets would buy them, however, the supermarkets insisted that the apples must be a certain size and a certain shape and they must be boxed, and all they were willing to offer was a miserable two dollars a box. Investigating, we found that the boxes themselves cost seventy-five cents each, truly not worth all that work and effort.

As this was lake country, three of them immediately nearby, Okanagan Lake, Kalamalka Lake and Swan Lake, we thought we would like to own a boat. Herb, another of our neighbours, was selling his. It was an eighteen-foot fibreglass model, with a sixty-five horsepower motor and seated a few people comfortably. There was a cover at the steering wheel end and it came with its own trailer, so we bought it. Up 'til that time, none of us knew much about motor boats. Allan and I had rowed on the Thames a few times, we rented boats at Bowness on the lagoon and rented boats when vacationing at lakes, but these were only rowboats. The chap where we found moorage took us around the lake a few times to help us to get the hang of it.

We had some wonderful times in that boat and we did some fishing in it. We'd pack a lunch and stay out on the lake for hours. Many friends and relatives enjoyed the boat; Gram, Muff-Anne and Megan, when Megan was just a baby and Janine and Paddie, Charlie and Cyril, two of Allan's uncles came to stay with us for a while. Being an ex-navy chap, Cyril enjoyed a cruise round the lake in the boat, but Charlie preferred to stay ashore.

In the middle of September, with both of the boys in school, Allan and I went to look at a piece of property. It was a half-acre property in Fintry on the mountain above Okanagan Lake. It wasn't serviced, but there was talk of bringing electricity and water to that area if enough people settled there. It was very quiet except for the birds around, a very nice piece of land and reasonably priced, so we bought it.

A small building company called *Northern Log* built a very nice cabin for us on the spot, running their tools with the aid of a generator. They had their headquarters somewhere in the United States. They are no longer in Vernon. I wonder if they went out of business?

We gradually put some furniture in the cabin. A studio lounge that we used in the early days of our marriage before we had a bedroom suite. An armchair that matched the studio lounge, a big coffee table that Allan had made from a door, many years before, a Franklin fireplace and a cook stove that used both propane and wood and also could be used for heating, and a couple of chests of drawers. We also built in a sink, complete with fittings and pipes and took some bedding there.

We had quite a number of barbecues at the cabin, and had established another place where we could spend time with relatives and friends sharing our cookouts, but in all of the time our cabin was on the mountain, *we* didn't stay overnight. One time Christopher and his friend Carlo spent a couple of nights there. I think they took food enough for a week and rather enjoyed it, but I'm sure they were glad to get back to civilization again.

Gram quite liked the time she spent at the cabin and many others visited with us; Alma and Margot, who were neighbours on East Vernon, Allan's cousins, Lila Mae and Joe, Nella and Frank, friends from Calgary. Janine made the trip with Paddie a few times. I really don't know what Timmie thought of the place, although the others certainly found it to be good fun.

There were other cabins in the area; one or two were quite large. Some of the owners came once a month to their places and others maybe only three or four times a year.

We parked our camper there on jacks, filled the water tank so that we had water for tea and coffee and doing dishes, and we could use the bathroom. There was a creek not too far distant.

In all of the hustle and bustle of 1981, moving, getting settled in, buying the cabin, Muff-Anne and Peter had a daughter on October 8th. Her name, Megan May, and she weighed only four pounds at birth. Three years later, on September 29, 1984, Megan May was joined by her new sister, Katlin Kit.

*My friends Mary and Jack some years later
celebrating their 60th wedding anniversary.*

*Revisiting #9 Dawson Place in London, the house
where I first met Allan during the war.*

Chapter 13

Other Horizons

Early in January of 1982 I began making plans for my second trip back to England. It had been twenty years since my last trip and I managed to get away in February.

I spent a few days with Mary and Jack, renewing acquaintance with people I had met twenty years earlier. We visited many places of historic interest. We spent time in Windsor Castle, went for a cruise on the Thames, saw the Eton boys coming from their famous college. We were on Dunstable Downs and watched the hang-gliders there. And I didn't miss visits with Martin and Steven, Mary and Jack's two sons, who had 'fought' over who was going to marry me when they grew up, when they were little boys. I had been reading a story to them at the time and in the course of the spree I got a puny punch on the nose. It was good to see them all again.

I stayed with Nan for a few days with most of the time spent with members of her family and friends. We reminisced about old times, for we had known one another for many years.

Phillip, Nan's next door neighbour, took us on some lovely drives. We went to Cotchford Farm close by Ashdown Forest, near the village of Hartfield in East Sussex. Ashdown Forest is wild and undeveloped much as it was when *Pooh* stamped around in it. *Pooh Country* is at the north end of a 6,400 acre preserve of moor and woodland. In August 1914 Lt. Harry Colebourn a vet officer with the 34th Fort Garry Horse of Manitoba travelled by train from Winnipeg to enroll in the Canadian Army Veterinary Corps in Valcartier Quebec. As he changed trains in White River in Ontario, he met a man with a bear-cub tied to the arm of the bench where he was sitting. The man, a trapper, had shot the cub's mother. Colbourne offered the man twenty dollars for the cub, who was quick to accept. In December 1914 the 2nd Brigade was preparing to move to France in great secrecy. While passing through London en route to France, Lt. Colbourne went to the London Zoo and asked them to care for the cub, while he was away, which he anticipated would be two weeks. It wasn't until 1918 that Lt. Colbourne, now a major, returned safely to London to visit "Winnie," as she had been dubbed affectionately by the workers at the zoo. Winnie was content and happy at the zoo, so Major Colbourne decided to leave her there, visiting her many times. She was now a big friendly bear who lived and played happily among thousands of friends both animal and human. She died peacefully on May 12, 1934.

A. A. Milne who wrote the book, *Christopher Robin*, took his son Christopher Robin to see the big friendly bear and he was quite taken with her. Christopher Robin asked his father if he would write a story for him about Winnie. He wanted Winnie to be called, "Winnie the Pooh." His father said, "Why Pooh?" Christopher Robin answered, "I don't know."
(I was wondering if it was 'cos bears are smelly!).

Nan lived in a little village called Otford in Kent, like so many picturesque villages dotted all over England.

Nan had a horse called *Oscar*, and an elderly English Pointed, called *Henry*. When Phillip took us on these drives, we always had to be back in time for *Henry* to be given his tea. We went to an old inn in Kent, which was well over two hundred years old, and had dinner there.

All too soon it was time to say goodbye to Nan and her family and visit a couple of days with Mary and George in Brighton who were members of the *National Trust Society,* which entitled them to visit many places of historic interest, all over England.

We went to the Peace Gardens, a spot I found quite enchanting, and to the Brighton Pavilion. It was built by George IV when he was Prince of Wales and Prince Regent. When he was only twenty-one, he and his morganatic wife, Mrs. Fitzherbert, bought a small farmhouse in what was then the village of Brighthelmstone. His penchant for sea bathing helped transform this small rural community into a mecca of high society over a period of almost fifty years from 1783 to his death in 1830. George IV continued to transform the simple home, first the farmhouse, which was incorporated into the Marine Pavilion. Architect Henry Holland then created a Neo-classical villa. In 1803 the Royal Stables were built in the Indian architectural style. Later sumptuous state rooms were added.

Somewhere in our travels, I remember we went to a place where the floor was made of cottage cheese!

Chichester Cathedral I found to be another one of those awe-inspiring places of worship that are found all over Europe. It was under restoration, as many of these old churches and cathedrals in Europe seem to be in this day and age. In Brighton there are so many places of interest and surprising little nooks where one can get refreshments on the waterfront or where one might dine more elegantly.

I went up to London for a few hours just to see Mummie Orsi's family; her son and daughter-in-law, Louisa and Johnny, and her grandchildren, Anna Marie and Johnny Jr. Her sisters, Ida and Rena, were there too. Mummie Orsi left this place some time ago, she was very sick and died of cancer, she was a very dear person. I was so glad to see so many dear friends again before I had to return to Canada.

1983 - A year that proved to be very anxious for us. Early in January Allan had to take the bus down to Vancouver General Hospital. He was to go before the Army Pension Board so that they could review his disability pension. The examining doctors discovered an aneurysm about ready to burst. They wanted to keep him in the hospital and operate immediately, but he told them he wanted to get back to his family in Vernon. When I met him at the bus station, he was so down and depressed. He had had more than his share of hospitals in his life and dreaded the thought of another hospital stay.

So it was arranged that he have the surgery, three days after the review, in Kelowna, a city about thirty miles from Vernon.

Alphonse, a good neighbour, took us to Kelowna and we checked Allan in at the hospital and they didn't lose much time performing the necessary surgery. Thank the good Lord all went well. They only kept him in the hospital for twelve days and advised him to rest completely for six weeks when he got home. The doctor did say, "You know, I've never done this operation on a non-smoker." Allan was quite a heavy smoker and many a time after that I threw cigarettes into the trash can.

Timmie left us in the fall to go to university. He stayed briefly with Muff-Anne and Peter in Stony Plain, and then moved down to Calgary to live with Gram. There he went to the University of Calgary for four years and studied the science of ground water. He hoped to get a job as a hydrologist, but that didn't quite work out. However, many years later he had a book published on ground water, *Ground Water Fluctuations in Alberta.* He switched to the field of computers and I think he might be called a computer scientist.

As Timmie was now away from Vernon, in Alberta, the work on the acreage was too much for Allan to handle because of his many health problems. I took care of the flower beds and veggie garden but there was quite a bit of other outside work to be done that I couldn't do.

Allan hadn't bounced back from that surgery the way he had hoped. So the big house with the acreage went on sale. It wasn't on the market for too long and we did take quite a loss, but it would have been futile to hang onto it.

We had a chap enlarge the condominium we had bought on Okanagan Lake. It was very small, around seven hundred square feet, just one very large room that took in living, dining, and kitchen area. A counter jutting out separated the kitchen from the living area. There was a very small bathroom with a shower and a very small bedroom. We had the construction fellow build out onto the patio area downstairs, and add a second storey covering the whole area. This cut down on the size of the patio quite a bit, but when the renovations were finished, it made the condo worthy of being called such, instead of remaining a tiny cottage.

We hadn't expected to be moving again so soon, but it was the wisest thing to do, in spite of the fact that moving was definitely not our favourite pastime. Downsizing our furniture and goods and chattels was not a happy pastime either, for we were moving from a three thousand square foot living area to a twelve hundred square foot area.

But we did get used to it, for one learns to adapt and there were some good and pleasant times down at the lake. It was so nice just to walk out the front door and be able to swim, and once or twice I was swimming as late as early October.

We fished quite a bit with the boat and I recall Allan canning some of the Kokanee salmon we had caught. Nothing we bought ever came close to it's succulent taste.

In our first years at the lake, there seemed to be a more stable quality to living and we knew everyone who lived there. Often Audrey, Grace, Janine and I would have tea together after our swim, or when the lake was too cold to swim we would go next door to the Lakeside Inn, have our swim and then jump into the hot tub. Oftentimes later in the evenings we'd have a fire on the beach. Marlene and Peter would be there, Grace and Jack, sometimes the Findlays, Audrey, Allan and I, and the boys, sometimes Janine and Paddie would come. It was friendlier in the beginning than it became later, with so many renters drifting in and out. We never knew who was living there or how long they would be there. As time went on, we became more and more disenchanted with living at the lake.

I had started singing with the Trinity United Church Choir while we still lived on East Vernon. I remember driving to church and coming down 25th Avenue in the winter, my little Pinto would start to fish-tail and my heart would pitter-patter. I would attend the 8:30 a.m. Mass at St. James, then slide down to Trinity on 27th Street, in time for the 10:00 a.m. service. I enjoyed the many years I sang with them and fortunately met some very nice people. I continued to sing with them after we moved to the lake, for it was a pleasant pastime.

Shortly after we moved, Allan became president of the strata council, 'cos no one else wanted the job. Allan didn't either, but as we were 'new' there, he thought he should do it! Our strata fees at that time were just thirty-two dollars a month, so there was no money in the kitty to pay for a lot of work that had to be done. All of the owners had to take part in the maintenance of the place. There were only twelve units in this strata and a few of the owners had their places rented out. Some of these owners didn't even live in town so it was impossible to enforce any hard and fast rule.

The people who rented were not expected to do any chores but the owners they rented from were supposed to see that the little gardens in front of their units were neat and tidy and the stretch of beach in front of their units was kept weed-free. But human nature being what it is ... the little gardens in front of the units were not always neat and tidy ... and the beach was not always free of weeds. And there were whispers, "He never does anything," or "She never does her share," and so on. It was, therefore, decided that Christopher would do the maintenance for a very nominal sum.

At one particular strata meeting, one of the owners suggested that those with two bathrooms should pay a higher strata fee. As we were the only unit with two bathrooms at that time, Allan came back with, "Do you think I pee more than you do?"

One of the girls in Trinity United Choir had informed me there was to be a reunion of war brides in Kelowna, giving me all the details. I talked it over with Allan, he agreed it might be a fun time, so we arranged to go.

I was hoping I might meet some of the girls I came over with on the *Aquitania*. I told Audrey about it as she was also a war bride. She said she would like to go. So Christopher and Janine took care of things at the lake while we were away.

It was a very nice affair and certainly worth the effort. There was a trip around the lake on the paddle wheeler the *Fintry Queen* with lunch included. We went to a wine and cheese party at a local winery and there was a formal dinner and dance on our last evening. I did not meet any of the girls I came over with on the *Aquitania* nor did Audrey. However, it was an interesting and enjoyable experience talking with other war brides from British Columbia as to how their lives turned out. We all agreed on one thing - Canada had been good to us, a grand country to live in! We came back to Vernon after our four day spree, ready to return to every day reality.

I had volunteered to help in the kindergarten in Okanagan Landing School, which turned out to be pleasant, and a time well spent. Looking back on those days brings back many emotions; gladness, to be part of a new generation, and sadness at the difficulties experienced by some of the children. I often now wonder at how those little kids came along later with their first experience with structured learning. Mostly though, remembering brings back many a smile!

1985 - Allan and I and Christopher went to England together. It was Allan's first and only trip back since the war years and Christopher's first.

Nan and Phillip met us at Heathrow. Our first stay was with Nan in Otford, not too far from Sevenoaks. Now referred to in a joking manner as 'One Oak'. Six of the seven oaks for which the town was named were destroyed in gales and storms some years previously.

Nan had prepared a meal for us but we were all overcome with jet-lag. We made an attempt to eat, but poor Allan fell asleep in the middle of a sentence. We felt rather bad for being such 'dull twits', but we made up for it the rest of the time we were there, at least we hope we did!

Later we spent a happy hour or so with Nan at a country fair.

We visited the ruins of the castle in Otford where Henry VIII held trysts with Anne Boleyn.

We went to Lullingstone Castle and saw the ruins of a nearby Roman villa. It must have been a very large villa belonging to a person of wealth.

Allan had seen quite a few places of historic interest

when stationed in England, and Europe through the war years. For Christopher though, it was all new and he took a keen interest in everything.

We decided to rent a car and we went to the village service station where they took care of the arrangements. I had to interpret for Allan, for it was quite a while since he had heard a Cockney accent! We were given a standard transmission Rover, but driving in England turned out to be not for Allan, he didn't enjoy it at all. Driving on the opposite side of the road and negotiating the roundabouts was a pain. We only kept the automobile a short while.

One evening Nan cooked a special dinner and invited her son Christopher, Evelyn her daughter-in-law, Jane one of her daughters, and Phillip her next door neighbour. During the meal Evelyn wondered how long Nan and I had known one another. We explained that it was many years.

"Oh, I see," she said, "you were young ladies together."

"I hope so," I exclaimed.

We eventually went up to London and stayed at a place in the Bayswater area with the illustrious name of *Leicester Court*. I had phoned earlier explaining the kind of accommodation we would need, including an en-suite.

We had a long wait while they were getting the room ready. When we were finally shown the room, we were most unhappy. The carpet was threadbare, both the window and the mirror were cracked. When I asked where the bathroom was, I was told, "The bathroom, she is down the hall." Of course, we paid top dollar, or top pound for the so-called suite.

In London we had a nice visit with Mamie and David, tea with Louisa and Anna Marie. Johnnie and Johnnie Jr. were working.

We took in a London bus tour. On the bus we met Lisa a girl from Washington, D.C. who was travelling alone. We made friends with her and she told us she had twin boys. We went to a couple of art galleries with Lisa who was a very nice girl. I think both Lisa and Christopher were quite in awe of Buckingham Palace.

We enjoyed a day with Mary and George in Brighton. Mary is quite an outstanding cook and after a most enjoyable lunch we went on a lovely drive around the area of Rottingdean, a very exclusive English girls' school.

We spent a couple of days in Hemel Hempstead and stayed at the *Midland Hotel*. As far as I know, although I may be wrong, there was nothing of historic interest there except a Corn Exchange where farmers of long ago came to sell their livestock and produce. One delightful thing Hemel Hempstead did have was a pond in the town centre with ducks on it.

Jack took us to Windsor where we saw the Windsor Greys, such lovely gentle horses that pull the royal carriages. They are stabled at the Royal Mews in London. Not too far from there, we went to a display commemorating Queen Victoria's Diamond Jubilee.

During our stay we had dinner with Mary and Jack, who were rather sad we didn't stay longer, a little visit with Ivy, a friend of Nan's I had met before, and tea with Susan, another of Nan's daughters. Nan's son, Christopher took us on a lovely drive. My own Christopher was taken with the friendliness of the English pubs. He had his first glass of bitter and quite enjoyed the pub food too. The evening before we left, Nan arranged for the local taxi to take us all the way to Heathrow Airport for a very nominal fee.

A lot was crowded into the time we were in England, and for me, it was good to see so many old friends again. For Allan and Christopher, they made new friends and had many new experiences. So we said our goodbyes to everyone and returned home to Canada. We had left our car at the airport in Kelowna, so there was no need to inconvenience anyone to meet us. The place didn't fall apart in our absence. Janine and our neighbour Margaret, kept things running pretty smoothly.

* * *

Christmas 1985. We seem to be the only ones at the beach. One or two may have departed for warmer climes, others to friends or relatives. Janine came for Christmas dinner which I don't remember cooking. All I remember of that day was that we sat around the fire on the beach and Janine played her recorder. It wasn't cold, the snow fell very gently, white and woolly, just the way my head felt. It was definitely the worst bout of flu I have ever had. I wouldn't repeat that experience again!

I tried very hard to keep the winter days from being empty by catching up on letter writing, putting snapshots in albums, cutting down on the mending, that's one chore that made me just delirious. I generally read more in the winter months and even did a little baking. Dropped in for chats with some of the neighbours such as Margaret and dear old Audrey.

Christopher and I would check on Margaret's cat *T.D.* if she were away for a couple of days. We'd feed him and give him water. She called him *T.D.* because she found him in the Terrace dump. Christopher was quite fond of that cat. He called it that 'baked' cat because the poor thing was very arthriticky. Christopher would have made a very good vet because of his genuine fondness for animals.

Allan and our neighbour Audrey loved to do crosswords, especially the more challenging ones, and they would compare notes. Allan and I tried our hand at making beer and wine. It turned out pretty well, but it was a little overpowering. Rather like 'white lightning'.

July 27th, 1986. Forty years since Allan and I were married in Paddington, a district of London. To celebrate we went out for dinner and when we returned we were greeted by the neighbours with champagne, a cake and flowers, quite a surprise. It was a lovely evening, and the time passed very pleasantly, chatting with all around the fire on the beach.

Later on Nella and Frank came to visit from Calgary in their mobile home and spent some time with us, Charlie and Cyril came with their trailer bringing Gram and Auntie Lil. We had quite a bit of company that year, a lot being from out of province.

The seasons soon moved into years. 1987 - Gram was

to be ninety years old on March 18th. Allan and I thought she should have a special party to mark the occasion, so it was arranged that I go to Calgary and talk things over with Gram. Although Gram was quite a retiring person and didn't like big fusses made, we made a list of all the people we thought she would like to come to the party.

All of the arrangements were made and I came back to Vernon where I busied myself with various springtime projects. I started little seedlings indoors of flowers and vegetables. I probably mentioned in my ramblings, that I really do enjoy gardening and I get very anxious for spring when the weather will be mild enough to put things into the ground. I can't speak with the same fervour about housework. I find it very ugly, obscene, and a vexation to the spirit. But if one wants to escape living in squalor, it is an absolute necessary evil. One afternoon a week I took part in pattern dancing. Allan accompanied me but he wasn't too interested, but he did like to watch. I was also helping at "my school" where boys and girls with varying degrees of mental handicaps were taught.

Soon it was time to make our way to Calgary again, this time by car. We left a few days before Gram's birthday, for there were preparations and other things to take care of. It was bitterly cold the day we left and the driving was quite hazardous, but we made it safe and sound.

Because there wasn't room for all the relatives and friends on just one side, the party was held in both sides of Gram's duplex. Doreen and Ron, Allan's cousins, opened up their side.

Gram received greetings from the prime Minister, several Members of the Legislature, and the Premier of Alberta. She enjoyed the relatives and friends and well-wishers and it was a very special day for her.

We stayed on in Calgary a few days visiting with Gram, Lorraine and Bernie, and Doreen and Ron, and Timmie who was living with Gram at that time. We were not to know when we said goodbye to Gram that our next visit with her would be in the hospital.

We returned to Vernon on a lovely spring day. The

175

Looking across Okanagan Lake from our condominium's front yard.
Tulips flourishing in the old boat that Jack Chapman gave me.

Allan sitting on the foundation in the
empty lot next to us at the cabin.

tulips and daffodils and spring flowers had pushed their heads well above the ground, although not quite time for putting in the bedding plants. Soon the speed boats and the Seadoos would be roaring all over the lake, and the wind-surfers would be zipping over the wave tops. Andrea, Timmie's friend, spent a few days with us that summer and she enjoyed the beach and the swimming in July.

I was busy taking care of the flowers I had planted in an old boat that my neighbour from number three, Jack Chapman, had given me. The annual plague of geese was tremendous and Jack came over to where I was working and said, "We must do something about these geese." I agreed with him. You couldn't walk on the lawn without being ankle deep in goose poo.

He told me that his friend's dog had had puppies and they were just about ready to leave the mother. He asked me, "If I brought one of the puppies to chase the geese, would you take care of it?" I told him yes, I would as long as someone could care for it when I was away. He went on to say that there was one male and three females in the litter and I told him that I would take the male. So it was arranged.

When Jack arrived with this little, snuffling, black scrap that just fitted on his hand, I didn't think I'd seen anything cuter. Jack explained that his mother was a pug and she was a smart little dog. His dad was a cocker spaniel and was awfully dumb. You couldn't help loving this little animal who was about seven weeks old. Even at that tender age, I rather think he took after his mother's smartness. For after we finished playing with him on the beach and made our way back to the condo he started to go into number three, but changed directions as if somehow he knew that number four was to be his home.

What to call this little black ball of nonsense. Christopher asked, "Can I call him Bob? I've always wanted a dog called Bob." We said okay then. Bob it was for Christopher, but I always called him Bobbie. It took him less than no time to learn his job of chasing the geese.

Before we got this little chap, Jack had asked the other

strata people how they felt about it. Everyone seemed in agreement that one dog messing on the lawn would be more acceptable than fifty or sixty geese doing the same thing. Later there were one or two dissenters crying, "I never agreed to it, the rules say 'no pets', nobody asked me," that kind of thing. But it all blew over and Bobbie became the best Canada goose chaser there ever was.

Allan was away at that time and I phoned to tell him about Bobbie's arrival. He said, "I thought we agreed on absolutely no more dogs." I told him we just couldn't resist this cute little creature. When Allan came home a few days later, he was quite in agreement.

Bobbie the goose dog.

August 22. A phone call from Timmie told us that Gram had been drying dishes, and had dropped one. Timmie had asked her if he could help, but Gram couldn't speak. Allan told him to quickly call an ambulance and then a priest.

Janine worked in Coquitlam and was visiting with us at that time and wanted to go with us to Gram's. We lost no time in getting on the road to Calgary where we immediately went to see Timmie. He was shocked by what had happened and certainly relieved to have us there.

We all went to see Gram in the hospital. It was so sad to see her lying there unable to communicate. She had always seemed invincible. Muff-Anne and Peter came down with the girls and stayed at Bankview. Soon the Haley's went back to Stony Plain. Christopher and I had to return to take care of things in Vernon, while Allan stayed on in Calgary.

Near the end of September Allan called saying that we should come to Calgary. We went and saw Gram and it was so sad. She hadn't spoken a word since she had had the stroke.

Gram died on September 29th, Katie's birthday. The service for her was held in Sacred Heart Catholic Church in Calgary and there were many in the church. She was a good person and well remembered. The priest who celebrated the Mass was from the Philippines and the family all seemed pleased with the way he conducted the service.

Returning to Vernon after a few days, a sad and subdued family with a special member gone, we were never the same. Christmas that year was a very quiet one, and rather unreal. Everyone was finding it very hard to come to grips with the loss of Gram and no one felt in a very festive mood.

My sister Mamie braving the elements in early
May 1961. Her son David sports her hat
which had blown off a few minutes earlier.

Chapter 14

Pilgrimage

1988 – Early in the year I received a phone call from my friend, Nan, in Kent. She began with, "Are you sitting down?" I knew instantly what she was going to tell me. She told me my sister, Mamie, had died in her sleep.

Whenever I think of Mamie, I feel very sad. She was an alcoholic. Nothing good seemed to happen in her life. It could have been our background, I don't know, I'm not a psychologist. Subconsciously, she may have been blaming her background and feeling bitter.

We were not close growing up, for she was quite domineering and controlling. But later, thinking about the way her life had turned out, I was very unhappy for her.

I didn't go to the funeral. There was only David, her son, and Nan, to say goodbye to her. The service must have been a very simple one. I think Nan must have taken care of any expense because Mamie's son, David, was not a responsible person.

I didn't ask Nan for any details at the time that she phoned. Maybe I just didn't want to hear that Mamie may have been buried in Potter's Field. And now, there is no one to remember her. Her husband, Arthur, had died sometime before. David, her son, I think would be rather indifferent and I don't know where he is today, and sadly, Nan has since gone.

It is the same with my father, who died almost forty years ago, no one to visit his grave. Why didn't I mention this before? I don't know. Was I trying to escape the memory of my past? Really, I don't think one can ever do that because it's always somewhere behind your mind. I don't know why on my many trips to England, I never asked Mamie where our Daddie was buried. And in retrospect it appears so callous and selfish, for I'm sure he did the best he could for us, with what he had. And that was oh so little.

I came across his 'In Memory' card stating that he died on May 18th, 1948, a little over a year after I came to Canada. But no matter how badly we feel, we can't go back and do things differently. I do hope my father's spirit knows these things.

Lonely Child
by *Mamie O'Neill*

She wander'd o'er the hills and vales,
Away from all the strife.
And as she walked, she weighed the scales,
Of her most lonely life.

No parents had she, no friends at all,
This little Child of nine.
But deep in her heart, there was a call,
To a far more heavn'ly shrine.

And as night fell, this lonely Child,
Lay herself down to rest,
And in the morning; dewy, mild,
She'd found eternal rest.

Tropic Nights
by *John Aloysius O'Neill*

Silver Moon on a Tropic Sea,
A million stars shine down on me.
The Sea is calm, The Night is still,
Except for notes of the Whip-poor-will.
My sandy bed, beneath a palm,
I lay me down, secure from harm,
With body tired, but spirit light,
I turn, and wish the World 'goodnight'.

1988 was the Marion Year in the Catholic Church when devotions and pilgrimages were made to Our Lady, the mother of Jesus. The Catholic Church in Vernon planned a twenty-four day pilgrimage to many countries in Europe. Allan and I had planned to make the pilgrimage, taking Christopher with us, but Allan's health wasn't good and he didn't feel up to making the trip. I think Christopher may have been a little anxious about it also, so I went alone.

There were forty-five of us signed up for the pilgrimage, with the majority from Vernon, a few others from Kamloops, Kelowna, and Armstrong.

Allan and Christopher drove me to the Kelowna airport to see me off there on the plane to Vancouver, it was very early in the morning.

Janine, who worked in Vancouver and her friend, Earl, came to the airport and we had breakfast together and then they accompanied me to where the group was assembled. As she liked to do, Janine had little gifts for me to cheer me on my way. A little mascot, reading materials, a special purse, and treaties in case I got hungry on the journey. At our parting, tears were never very far away.

The priest, Father David, who had planned this pilgrimage, had been brought up as a Baptist. He went into the seminary much later than most priests do, as he was earning a living as a chef, indeed a very good one. I think he may have been around forty when he was ordained. There was also a priest, Father Carlos, from the Philippines who went along as well.

It was quite a feat escorting forty-five people to foreign parts for twenty-four days. Trying to keep them all relatively content, if not happy for all that time, took quite a bit of ingenuity.

For even though we were all of the same religion, we certainly were not all alike. There were many petty grievances and bickering that went on such as; "My roommate smokes." "The one I'm partnered with snores." "My roommate makes noises in the middle of the night." "She's always up and down to the bathroom." "My roommate drives me mad." "She's always putting things in little bags and putting rubber bands around them." And so it went on.

Arriving at the various hotels, the guide on the tour would tell us the numbers of the rooms we were allotted. Almost everyone in the group shared a room with another. More than one person, sometimes a little too sharply would ask me, "Why do *you* always get a room on your own?" And I would reply simply, "Because I paid for it."

Our first stop was Rome with a welcome banquet awaiting us and all of the ladies were presented with a red rose. I don't remember the food they served but there was wine, and it was a very warm affair. Before dinner we sang a Grace to the tune of *Edelweiss*, a lovely start to the pilgrimage. As we were leaving the restaurant, my rose hooked itself onto the seat of the pants of the man in front of me. It was rather embarrassing untangling it.

The hotel they had chosen for us was quite nice, in the centre of things with many little cafés and souvenir shops around. Even the hotel had its own souvenir shop.

I went with a couple in the group for a walk about taking in the local colour.

We had to rise very early the next morning to have an audience with the Pope. Only a little after eight in the morning, we were outside waiting to get into the Vatican,

184

and the sun was very hot, many of us used our maps for protection from the sun and after a long wait, we entered the Vatican. There were many groups there, crowds of dignitaries and officials of the Vatican.

The Pope celebrated the Mass and gave everyone Communion. I couldn't help thinking that when the Pope came close; he seemed to have a saintly aura about him. At that time he had such stamina, whenever I see him on television today, I feel very sad that he's so frail but still carrying on his duties.

The people were not presented to the Pope individually, that would have been impossible. A Vatican official would name the group and where they were from, and then the Pope would bless them. I was able to get a very good close-up snap of the Pope, for Father Carlos, the priest from the Philippines, cleared a way for me right at the front.

We were taken on a tour of the Sistine Chapel and its wondrous artworks. Everyone who enters the Chapel must obey the signs, *silencio*. We could have spent the entire twenty-four days around the Vatican, so much to see. The churches we did see in Rome were magnificent and, as are so many churches in Europe, under restoration.

We visited the Coliseum and down in the catacombs where thousands of early Christians and martyrs were buried, we met a teenage girl who was separated from her group and was quite scared. I think we made her feel better because we told her that the early Christians couldn't hurt her, as they were all dead.

We visited the *Three Fountains* and as tradition demands threw in money.

On the subject of money, many cafés would not let you sit down unless you spent a thousand lire or so, about one United States dollar. For example, I became separated from a friend in the group, so I went into a café for a cup of tea. I paid my dollar for the tea as well as my dollar to sit down. After five minutes or so a waiter came and cleared away my tea things. I told him I had paid to sit there and that he could check with the cashier. When he did, she said I hadn't paid. I was very upset with this experience and not too impressed with that particular café in Rome.

We travelled to Florence and saw the statue of David, went to an art gallery and on the streets there was a procession honouring John the Baptist.

We took a gondola on a canal in Venice and found a glass blowing factory so very hot that some of us couldn't stay in there too long.

The guide on our coach, a very nice Italian chappie, had quite a sense of humour. Always before leaving the hotel where we had stayed, he would stand at the front of the coach and say, "Has everyone got their purses, their sweaters, their jackets, their cameras. Has everyone got their teeth?" He tried to cover everything and asked if we had turned in our keys. It did get very tiresome being constantly on the alert and standing shotgun over one's possessions.

One day Father David told us he was going to take us to a convent where he had stayed when he was studying in Italy. We had been on the coach a very long time and I know the feeling among many of us was, "Who cares, I'm tired, I want to get off this coach, I want to have a bath and relax," but when we reached the place a lovely surprise awaited us to cheer our spirits. A welcoming spread was prepared by the dear nuns with a variety of sandwiches, coffee, tea, juice, and also home baked goodies. Best of all, we didn't have to watch over our possessions.

Throughout the coach journey the guide would announce, "We will stop for lunch, or we will stop for a coffee, or we will stop to wash the 'ands." One time my seat companion was a nun, Sister Kathleen. When I saw the toilet facilities I exclaimed, "I can't use those." It was just open drains in a tiled floor, but she said, "Well, I have to." I didn't think there was anything that primitive left in the Western world in 1988.

During another of those comfort stops the washroom attendant chased after one of the ladies of our group because she failed to leave a few lire in her kitty. The lady in question was certainly not familiar with this custom.

We went to Assisi, where Saint Francis the lover of

birds and animals and all wild life was born. I hope that I'm not wrong in saying that he is the patron saint of birds and animals and all wild life. Our guide was from the monastery in Assisi. He was from New York and we learned from him that Saint Francis was a small, slight, man.

In Pisa, where the famous Leaning Tower is, a couple of the 'girls' from our group and I use that word advisedly, decided to climb the stairs to the top of the tower. I don't think they made it.

The tour took us to France and we were in Nimes and visited the famous Nimes Cathedral, another splendid example of the architecture of places of worship all over Europe, and went to Nice very briefly. These two towns gave me the feeling of being light-hearted. There were some bright department stores and when one stopped for a coffee or a snack, people were warm and courteous. I remember it rained while we were in Nice.

When we arrived in Marseilles we were doubly warned to keep a close eye on our possessions, as in all port towns, one had to be wary. However, I did like Marseilles, the scene at the harbour was an artist's dream.

Wherever we stopped on the tour, one of the priests, usually Father David, would say a Mass in the local church. We were in so many churches they blur in my memory.

I tried jotting down events in a journal along the way, but as the tour moved along very fast, and I didn't want to make the journal a chore, the jotting became rather haphazard. When we moved to where we live now, I couldn't find that journal.

There was a candlelight procession to Our Lady in Lourdes, hundreds took part, maybe thousands, I'm not sure, hymns to Our Lady were played over the P.A. system with everyone joining in the singing. We spent time at the grotto of Our Lady, where Bernadette saw the visions of Our Lady, and were able to take away holy water from the grotto. Bernadette Saubirous was born in Lourdes in 1844 and she didn't enjoy good health. Her father was a miller and his was a poor family. She saw the first of eighteen visions in 1858. She died in 1879.

I liked Lourdes very much and had the impression that it wasn't very large with a small population. With all the priests, religious, and pilgrims visiting from many countries year round, it was hard to tell.

One evening in Lourdes the rain came down in torrents. A lady from our group didn't show up for dinner. One of the priests and a man from the group went to look for her and brought her back safe and sound, but they were all very, very, wet. One silly little thing stays in my mind about Lourdes. One of the ladies in the group had seen a handbag in a souvenir shop that she really liked but was undecided about buying it. I went with her after dinner to look at the bag and told her, "Yes, it was very nice, but it did seem very costly." But she bought it anyway.

In Monte Carlo we saw those places where fortunes were won and lost on the spin of a wheel. Where many a fool, even the not so foolish, and his money were soon parted. We toured the palace at Versailles and saw the palace in Monaco. We were in Liechtenstein and then Luxembourg hearing Mass celebrated in one of the churches. It seemed we were only long enough in those two places to get a glimpse of the local scene.

On the tour there was no shortage of souvenir shops, on many occasions the guide would let us off the leash and leave us to our own devices. He would say, "We will meet back here at such-and-such a time or under the clock, or by the statue. " A lady in our group named Maria was always late. One of the chaps in the group would sing, *How do you solve a problem like Maria."* She loved to shop and was an expert at throwing money away. In Venice she bought a carafe and liqueur glasses for a thousand dollars and I bet she has never used them. One day Maria was again late, so when we were going back to the hotel the guide decided we'd leave without Maria. She wasn't non-plussed, she simply took a taxi and laughed it off. I don't think she was any more punctual at the end of the tour than she was at the beginning.

We found Switzerland to be a wondrously clean country. Our guide explained that anyone caught littering would be given a warning and if caught again would be fined. We also learned that Switzerland would be more than ready to defend itself should any hostilities arise, having the wherewithal to do so kept in readiness underground.

I felt very sad looking at the Lion of Lucerne. It is carved into the face of a rock. The monument was designed by Thorwaldson and dedicated in 1821 to the memory of the Swiss guards who fell defending Louis XVI during the attack of the mob on the Paris Palace, August 10th, 1792. The lion is dying, there is a broken spear in his heart. His paw is resting on a shield with a fleur-de-lis motif.

We arrived at our hotel in the mountains in Austria late in the afternoon with just time to freshen up and get ready for dinner. Some of us had a look around the village after dinner. We were up early the next morning attending Mass in another of Europe's splendid churches.

In Spain we were taken to see a very large arena where bullfights were once held. We were told that they no longer had bullfights, they were more like bull games. In the evening we went to a nightclub and it was fun. Some of the chaps in our group would applaud each act with an, "Olé."

In Rome waiting for the plane to Canada, I recollected on what a whirlwind tour it had been. I can't say it was a relaxing time, but it certainly was interesting. As we touched down in Vancouver, there was a chorus of "Ole's."

Allan and Christopher were waiting for me at the Kelowna airport. I didn't realize how tired I was until I stopped bustling. I tried to tell them a little about the journeys, but my thoughts kept bumping into one another, and I thought the story would best be told later. It always takes a while to get over the jet-lag.

* * *

Allan and I had planned a seven day cruise to Mexico, but then Allan who didn't care for traveling very much decided he didn't want to go, so I went alone. The cruise was fine but it would have been nicer if Allan had been with me.

The people I was seated with in the ship's dining room were very nice and I made friends with some. There is much too much food on a cruise ship and one feels very guilty when there is so much hunger in the world, especially when seeing Mexico's children, some as young as four years old, begging. A guide on a bus tour of Puerto Vallarta told us not to give money to the beggars for it would just perpetuate the begging, but one would have to very, very cold-hearted to ignore them. Another thing that distressed me was seeing the way some of the poor lived in large cardboard boxes with corrugated aluminium for a roof. Some of our most modest homes would seem like palaces to them.

We were taken to a brickyard up in the Sierra Mountains where they made bricks the old fashioned way with mud. The open-air market was quite fun, you could buy just about anything there. We took a mini cruise around Cabo San Lucas and there were many seals on the rocks, I must say, it was very smelly. While in Puerto Vallarta we were entertained by Mexican dancers and I had my first taste of tequila. We were introduced to an American who seemed to be well known to tourists as he liked to show them the house he bought for eight hundred dollars and fixed up.

There was no shortage of things to do, entertainment every night, an exercise room, beauty shop, a library, craft classes, ballroom dancing and a swimming pool.

The seven days was over very fast. Janine met me at Vancouver Airport and I stayed a couple of days with her before returning to Vernon. Allan was at the Kelowna Airport to meet me and it was good to see him, he looked quite anxious and rather tired. He was glad that I was home and so was I. It was time to clear up my flower garden and my little veggie patch.

That year Timmie received his Bachelor of Science degree. We attended the convocation in Calgary, feeling very happy for him and proud, as were all the other parents.

Chapter 15

Jerusalem

1989 - Allan and I planned to go the Holy Land and both hoped he would feel up to the journey.

Christopher was twenty-one on the 31st of March. How did that happen? It seemed such a little while ago he was playing Superman and Batman and his 'stupid Ace games' with Paddie, as brother Timmie called the game. And now he was six foot one and his interest in art all consuming. I hoped that he might get into the field of graphic art. Christopher was not living at home any more, though in Vernon again after staying a few months with Timmie and Patricia in Calgary, and we saw him quite often. We missed him very much and we were sad to see him go.

Now it was just Allan and I and Bobbie, the little goose dog, and Boris the wild cat who still sat on the long box beneath the front window waiting to be fed. Christopher had made him a little insulated house from an orange crate that sat on top of the long box that Allan made as a catch-all for many odds and ends. Boris quite loved his home.

Allan and I tried to go to the cabin at least once a week, the odd time staying overnight. In the good weather we would tend to the lawn and the garden and in inclement weather tend to things inside the cabin and we often popped in to see Del and Bob next door. Our little dog Bobbie didn't like the cabin very much even though he could run free and there were acres to explore. I think what he missed was greeting everyone at the lake house as they came home. He just loved that and he would be greeted in turn and fussed over. There were only two people at the lake who weren't friendly to him and he just couldn't understand it.

Allan enjoyed fishing from the dock, the fish weren't

too plentiful but he enjoyed watching the activity on the lake.

There was some silly dissension for a while over us feeding the birds and Boris and the other wild cats. Allan would always happily give Boris the fish that he caught. We told those cold-hearted dissenters that we couldn't see those dumb creatures go hungry, which may have shamed them because we didn't hear too much from them after that.

The time for our trip to Israel drew near and sadly Allan felt not up to going. It was arranged that Christopher stay with Allan and I went alone. It was most disappointing, but the group and the guide were very friendly and I must say, it was an extremely interesting tour.

In Israel we were taken to the location that may have been Golgotha, the place of the crucifixion and also to the tomb believed to have belonged to Joseph of Aramathea where Jesus was buried. We walked the way of the Cross and I thought the Chapel of the Flagellation was the saddest stop of all.

We were taken to where the Last Supper may have been held and to the Garden of Gethsemane. The garden was much smaller than I thought it would be. We were served St. Peter's fish one day for lunch. I couldn't determine what kind of fish it was.

We were in Bethlehem where Jesus was born, at Cana where Jesus turned water into wine. We put our messages into the Wailing Wall in Jerusalem and while there we saw a young chap celebrating his Bah Mitzvah. There were a few beggars hanging around the square.

We were taken to the Sea of Galilee and we swam in the Dead Sea popping around like corks. We were at the River Jordan, where I believe John the Baptist baptized Jesus. I was disappointed to find that this body of water was a brackish green and not running clear.

In the synagogue of the Hadassah Hebrew University Medical Centre in Jerusalem we saw the stained glass windows of Marc Chagall. The Synagogue was dedicated on February 6th, 1962 as part of Hadassah's Golden Anniversary celebration.

While visiting two or three synagogues the men in the group had to put on yarmulkes, little skull caps made of thin cardboard; there was always a supply of disposable yarmulkes near the entrance of the synagogue for the use of visitors.

We viewed the Dead Sea Scrolls. In 1947 a shepherd boy going after one of his sheep that wandered into a cave, found the scrolls in a large earthenware jar, the oldest Biblical records ever found. The Scrolls trace the history and daily lives of the mystical Essenes - a Jewish sect that fled Jerusalem two thousand years ago. The scrolls prompted excavations, which subsequently revealed the complexity of Essene life. Many of the scrolls are displayed at the Shrine of the Book of Israel Museum in Jerusalem.

We had a short tour of a diamond factory. I don't know if 'factory' is the right term, anyway, where they were polishing and cutting diamonds. Israel is one of the foremost countries in the world, so we were told, in the cutting and polishing of diamonds.

Near the Westbank at that time we had rocks thrown at our tour bus and we were a bit alarmed, but the guide told us it was just teenagers getting into a bit of mischief and no one was hurt.

We spent time in a Muslim mosque. There was no seating in those places of worship but the floors were covered with what appeared to be expensive carpeting - Turkish carpets, Indian carpets, and maybe even some Axminster carpets. There was an assistant guide with us that day and she stayed outside the mosque with our bags and cameras and things, for we were not allowed to take these into the mosque.

We all stayed overnight in a kibbutz and were treated wonderfully. The food was so good, and the rooms so comfortable and clean. We visited the Holocaust Museum, the saddest place in all of Israel. Such compelling remembrance of one of history's most terrible crimes.

In the cities, especially Jerusalem there were many narrow streets that were no more than alleys but they had little shops tucked away in them. Stone steps led up from the shops to what appeared to be living quarters above. While wandering through these alleyways we would often see small dark-eyed children, barefoot, coming down the steps just watching us strangers who had come to their country. It wasn't unusual to see small groups of men in their prayer shawls with their prayer boxes on their foreheads praying on the streets of Israel, they were very devout. And it wasn't unusual wandering through the alleyways and the bazaars to have to stand aside when a man with his donkeys or a shepherd with his sheep, or a goat-herd with his goats came by.

Saturday, our last day in Israel, the Sabbath and everything was shut down. Orthodox Jews do not work on the Sabbath - not even elevator operators in hotels. Of course, one could always operate the lifts. I still had one or two things to buy as souvenirs, but where to go?

So I went in search of a shop run by someone of another faith, and I did find one tucked away in one of those alleys. I wasn't sure if it was wise to go there all alone. No one knew I was there. What if I had been kidnapped and held for ransom, who would pay to set me free? Maybe I had read too much or seen too much on television about the mysteries of the Mid-East and the Far-East.

Years ago we had been baffled by those Charlie Chan movies with tales of the Orient. How mysterious it all was to us. But now many years later I knew that people are people, and wherever one went the world over, there were people good, bad, and indifferent.

I came away from that shop very pleased with myself and my purchases, for the merchant there seemed the kind of chap you had to bargain with, and so I did.

My next little adventure that day was going in search of a light lunch. I found a tiny little café, went in and asked to have some tea and a grilled cheese sandwich. I was the only one there. The owner may have been Muslim, he was very kind and obliging and he brought me a grilled cheese sandwich made in a pita bread. After lunch I went back to the hotel to pack then went down to the lounge and had coffee with a couple from our group. There was a nice farewell dinner for us that evening.

We had to be at the airport at three-thirty in the morning, so none of got very much sleep that night. There was coffee for us, also juice and toast and rolls. No one was hungry but we were glad of the coffee.

Security was very tight at Ben Gurion Airport. Once on the plane, it wasn't long before they served breakfast and it was an overpowering one, especially for someone who never normally eats breakfast. My seat companion was a very large chappie who overflowed onto my seat. He asked me, "Was I not going to eat my breakfast?"

I said, "Oh no, I'm not hungry."

"May I have it then, please?"

"Certainly," I said.

How happy I was to be back in Canada, but I was very glad that I took that tour of Israel. It was most interesting and it did bring forth many emotions to be in places where Jesus and his Disciples were. To walk the way of the Cross, to visit Bethlehem, to be on Mount Sinai and the Mount of Olives. To visit the Holocaust Museum. There was sadness and gladness, and wonder too at all we saw and experienced while in Jerusalem.

Allan and Christopher were there to meet me at Kelowna Airport, with dear little Bobbie. He didn't like suitcases, for he knew when suitcases appeared that someone from his little world would be leaving, and how would he in his little mind know that they would be coming back, so whenever I went on a trip I would tell him, "Bye-bye Bobbie, be a good boy, see you soon." He would never say goodbye, he would turn his head away from me, but when I came back, when I was in the car, he would jump on my lap, wag his tail, and cover me with doggie kisses. Poor old Boris, the wild cat, died while I was in Israel; Allan said he became quite sick before he died.

I expected that I would have been back in Vernon in time to sing in the Carol Festival with the United Church Choir, but it would have been too much of a rush

* * *

1990 - The years had whipped by very fast. By this time, I didn't make New Year's resolutions any more; I just hoped that I could do the best with each day that came along. I thought I did very well to stop smoking in 1969, after about eighteen tries, and I used to smoke Buckingham's, twenty-five a day. We didn't know then just how dangerous it was to smoke.

That year Allan and I would have been married for forty-four years. Sometimes it seemed a very long time and sometimes it felt like only yesterday when we began our life together. There had been glad times and sad times, anxious times, and many ups and downs. Four grown children and four grandchildren, we were still facing life's ups and downs together.

Allan had had such high hopes and plans for the future of all the things we would be able to do when he retired in 1979, but to quote Robbie Burns, "The best laid schemes o' mice an' men gang aft a-gley." Since not enjoying the best of health, many of Allan's plans were not realized.

We went by bus to Reno in the spring, thought it might be fun to play the nickel and dime one arm bandits. We stopped for an overnight stay just across the border and Allan had a very bad turn. I felt that we should return home but Allan wouldn't hear of it. The people on the bus were very helpful and Allan did feel a little better after a good night's rest.

In Reno we stayed in a lovely room at the *Flamingo* and the food was very good. There was some alarm and a bit of panic one evening caused by a mild earthquake, which registered around four on the Richter scale. People were coming out of their rooms in their housecoats, some of the ladies with curlers in their hair. It happened around nine in the evening and many of the group, tired after the long bus ride were getting ready to retire for we were to leave early the next morning. Allan had dozed off on the bed and was rudely awakened when the bed started shaking. It was over in seconds and things were back to normal with no damage done, at least not in our area, and we hoped not anywhere else.

Allan was not able to take any of the side trips that were included in the tour. We went to Lake Tahoe and that was a nice pleasant afternoon. We were at *Baileys*, quite a well known casino. It seems to me I heard that the staircase in *Baileys* was used in a scene from *Gone With The Wind*, unless I imagined it and I am full of hot air.

There were one or two smaller casinos we went to and they gave us a roll of nickels to start our gambling fever. Allan did play the machines a little, but as there is no comfortable seating in a casino, he preferred sitting in a chair in the lounge watching life's passing parade, or near a window observing the comings and goings of the street scene. I did some walking around, taking in a little of the local scene of Reno which is a very, very, busy place. The casinos must provide employment for a large percentage of the workforce in Reno.

We had a nice little party on our last night in Reno and the next morning it was off home again to rejoice in our winnings or grieve over our losses. Allan and I came out just about even, winning around one hundred and fifty dollars each on one play and many smaller wins.

The day after we returned to Vernon I made an appointment for Allan with the doctor. He was put on an oxygen machine right away. He was already on several inhalers and needed much medication to help him breathe easier.

I had read about a new operation that was being performed on people with lung problems. I asked the doctor if that could be done for Allan, he told me his lungs were too far gone and it couldn't be done. The start of Allan's problems had begun in the '40's after he had the surgery for high blood pressure. His lungs had become infected and he developed pleurisy and, of course, being a smoker certainly didn't help the condition.

And so he had another big adjustment to make, living with the need for oxygen. I supposed that only a person who had been there knew how uncomfortable and depressing that would be. I must say here, however, in all of his sickness there was no self-pity, only frustration that he couldn't do relatively normal things.

Among Allan's plans when he retired, was to go again to Paris where he was during the Second World War and I would go with him. Though I had been in France, I had never been to Paris. He also wanted to go back to England to where he had been stationed during the war and to visit some of his army buddies in Eastern Canada, and the United States. Allan and Al Gow, a Calgary Court House friend, talked about panning for gold when they retired. I actually bought him the gold pan, but these things also didn't come to pass.

Nevertheless, we managed one trip to England a few years earlier and we did get to Reno, plus many trips to Calgary to see Gram and Timmie. We enjoyed journeys to Edmonton and to Stony Plain to see Muff-Anne, Peter, and the girls, and I do think if Allan were in better health he may have enjoyed travel more. He knew that I enjoyed travelling and said he would still like me to go even though he couldn't.

Later that year I went to Greece with a group of twenty-five others. We saw the Parthenon. We were taken to a very large amphitheatre in the open air and I was not sure if they still used it, but it seemed to be very well preserved. I imagined that quite a bit of upkeep work was done on those historical sites. We went to a few of the little coastal fishing villages and we were taken on a lunch-time boat cruise.

At a Greek Orthodox Church I couldn't help but smile at a notice outside in English that went something like, *"Please to be respectful, and no nudity please inside church."* It probably meant no shorts for anyone, and that the men had to wear a top. It goes without saying, the women certainly should!

We stayed in Athens and once or twice I didn't feel like eating at the hotel and went along to a little nook not too far from the hotel. They served the most delicious cheese pies; I guess it was feta cheese. A very friendly little cat came to sit near me while I was there; it was very small, and

Here I am on a warm sunny day in Greece, however, in a few minutes clouds rolled in and the temperature dropped making us all miserable.

very thin. I offered it some of the cheese pie; it didn't eat it, so I guess it wasn't hungry. When we saw other cats in Greece they were all small and thin. Maybe they are a special breed raised only Greece.

The tour took us to many ruins of ancient temples and other buildings of historic importance. Once when we started out in the morning it was a beautiful day, warm and sunny, everyone wore shorts and summer attire, but suddenly the weather turned cold and windy and very dark. We were at quite a high elevation and the guide was busily telling us the history of the ruins of an ancient temple. However, I don't think any of the group was too interested in what he was saying; we were all too cold and wanted to get back to the hotel. Just then a lovely friendly dog came along, put it's head on my knee begging to be petted, so that was a bright spot in that rather dreary time.

I was the only one in the group travelling alone, some of the group asked me if I was nervous or apprehensive about travelling alone. My answer was that I couldn't really say that I was blasé, but that I had taken quite a few trips alone, sometimes with a group, sometimes staying with friends in another country. In Greece there was one incident that startled me quite a bit when I was coming back from the little restaurant nook I mentioned. I was on a main, well-lighted street, that particular evening when a rather wild looking man approached me speaking in Greek in a very agitated way. I scurried off as quickly as I could. I realized afterwards he must have had a mental problem.

I had my introduction to ouzo during our final dinner in Greece. I found it very different and quite overpowering.

Marjorie, one member of our group, had told me that she had a mother named Louise in Vernon who lived alone and loved company and asked if I would go and see her? I agreed provided that her mother wanted the company. Louise and I met later and I still see her now and again today. (When I first met Louise, she was living independently in a senior housing complex, but now she is living in a care home. The same home that Janine worked in a couple of times a week, putting the residents through mild exercises and various activities).

Home again from abroad and on Canadian soil. Allan liked to hear what happened while I was away in other countries, but I do feel it rather tired him.

Janine drove up from Coquitlam for the Christmas and New Year holiday. I cooked the *festive beast* and all the other stuff that went with him and we had a pretty good Christmas and New Year, and Timmie came out with Andrea, and they stayed a few days.

Back in Vernon, visiting Louise, Marjorie's mother.
I had met Marjorie on my trip to Greece.

Chapter 16

Travelling On

Springtime 1991 - Daffodils and tulips and other spring flowers appeared to make the heart glad. My roses came through the winter and I planted seeds in my little veggie patch.

Allan liked to watch the game shows on television, and as I mentioned, Allan and Audrey, a friend at the lake, used to compare notes on crosswords, especially the difficult ones, one of the puzzles came from the New York Times. Allan kept up with the news and there were one or two favourite shows that we watched together and a couple that he watched with Christopher. He remained interested in events going on around the world even though his physical activities were very limited.

He would take a chair out on the dock and fish even though he didn't catch anything, it was a change of scene and it got him out of the house. Sometimes he might water my little flower garden in the front and my veggie patch. He kept all the books, wrote all the cheques and saw that all the bills were paid. He would prepare the veggies for meals and he would do the folding on wash-day.

Often he would complain about being useless and that he hated the idea of doing nothing. He got very distressed at these times and I do hope when I recounted to him all that he did manage to do that he had less negative feelings about himself.

In 1991 I went to Fatima in Portugal where the three children saw visions of Our Lady. The oldest of these peasant children Lucy de Santos, was barely ten, and her cousins, Jacinta Marto was seven, and her brother Francisco Marto was nine. They first saw the vision of Our Lady in a pasture north of Fatima on May 13th, 1917. Our Lady promised to meet them on the same day every month until October.

There were six meetings in all. Only the three children were at the first one, but there were seventy thousand men, women and youths, from all walks of life, and every corner of Portugal at the last.

For six months these three little children had withstood scorn, police threats, mental torture at the hands of the authorities, and anger from their own families. Who was there to pay any attention to three peasant children who could neither read nor write? The general feeling was that they were rather backward. Jacinta and her brother both died within three years after the visitations. Their cousin Lucy, lived on to enter a convent when she was old enough and the rest of her life was spent as a religious.

I stayed in a convent in Fatima. The priest in residence was a Father Martin. The staff and Father Martin were all very kind to me while I was there and I was the only guest. Father Martin told me of an elderly lady in her eighties who used to drive from Spain every year for a short retreat.

Father Martin and I had our meals together. The food was good but very plain. I think they may have been on a very strict budget. One day he asked me if I could make bread pudding. There were a lot of hard rolls he didn't want to throw away. The ingredients he gave me were quite meagre to what I used at home, for example, two ounces of raisins. When I said that I would need some shortening, they gave me beef fat. They had some brown sugar, but they didn't have any mixed fruit. I used some orange and lemon peel and some apples. Though I'd never made a bread pudding with so few ingredients, everyone seemed to enjoy it. Father Martin told me that I was welcome to have coffee any time of the day, and there was usually pie or cake to accompany the coffee, but most of the time I had to decline because there was always enough food at meal time.

Father Martin came from the United States. Martin was his Christian name, and he explained that his Polish surname was just too hard to pronounce. As I write this many years after, Father Martin and I are still good friends.

I don't remember the church in Fatima having any traditional pews, mostly benches. That church was not very ornate compared to other churches in Europe. On the floor in the church in Fatima there were two slabs made of either marble or granite; one in memory of Jacinta and one in memory of her brother, Francisco Marto. I think their cousin Lucy was still in a convent in Portugal and certainly getting along in years when I was in Fatima. I was glad I went and now I know a little more than I did before about the visionaries of Fatima and hoped to read more about them. I find the story very interesting and I am sure many others would also. One thing I did notice though that many of the residents of Fatima, especially the older ones and especially women, were not averse at pushing people out of the way to get to Communion before them. You might say that their social graces were very few.

Timmie had mentioned that Father Hilling, a priest from Sacred Heart Church in Calgary would be in Fatima at the same time as I was. I got in touch with him and we had coffee together. During our pleasant chat he told me he had hopes that Timmie might enter a seminary and become a priest. Of course that didn't happen.

On my last day in Portugal, I had to be at the airport very early the next morning. Father Martin said an early Mass, a very short one, and I made the responses as there was no one else there. He made breakfast for me, and it was around four o'clock in the morning.

He arranged for a taxi to take me to the airport at Lisbon. There was no other kind of transportation and Fatima was some distance from Lisbon. On the long ride to the airport, I thought about the time I asked a lady for directions in Fatima to a certain place, she said, "I cannot tell you, but I will put you there for I have a car." I thought her speech was quite amusing but I was glad 'she put me there'.

I was always so glad to be home again and not the only one to be glad. Allan was always so happy when I came back from a trip. He told me that Christopher was very good to him while I had been away. He'd walk a little way around the area with him, not too far, for Allan would get out of breath. They managed with the cooking not too badly and kept the house in some kind of order and the laundry was done.

I regaled them with stories of Portugal until they started to get bored. I told them how apprehensive I was when a policeman came up to me when I was sitting in a little park area quite near the Fatima church. It was warm and sunny. I had put my camcorder and my tote bag down a little way away from me and the policeman told me, "Madam, you must not do that. You must keep things near you. Maybe someone take it." I thanked him, glad that I wasn't breaking any local rules.

I told them that Father Martin had lived near Norman Rockwell at one time and he said he was a very nice man. Told them about the church, the processions, and the lady who 'put me there', until I thought they'd heard enough.

I went to Israel again that year, just for a short time, because I didn't want to leave Allan for too long. I had to change airplanes at Toronto and was stopped by security. While my luggage was searched I was questioned at length. They wanted to know why I was going to Israel again, did I have friends there? Did I have relatives there? No, not the safest place to go. They may have thought that I was some kind of subversive or, on going through my luggage and finding my little teddy bear, that goes with me on all my travels, that perhaps I was smuggling. And when I thought about it later; what better person to do it, than this small, benign looking lady. They asked me if I would like to sit down and I told them, "No, I'm not feeble yet, but I may be by the time you are finished with me." Anyway, I didn't miss my plane.

There was no one to meet me when I arrived at Ben Gurion Airport. I had the name of the hotel where the agent had booked me so I got a taxi and made my way to the hotel at my own expense hoping the guide would be in the same hotel. But upon enquiring discovered that he wasn't, and he didn't appear until later the next morning. So far I wasn't very pleased with the way things had gone and I resolved to change my travel agent the next time I took a trip. To that point the heavens weren't smiling on me.

There weren't nearly as many in the group on the second tour as were on the first one I took in Israel. There were only two others staying at my hotel, the others were staying at three different hotels. The guide collected us all and we set off in a rather large van, a motley crew of about twelve souls.

We went to many of the places as on my first trip to Israel. This time I wanted to observe more of the every day life in Israel and wander in old Jerusalem among the bazaars and the shops in those funny little alleys. I had found them quite fascinating. Imagine in this twentieth century, people are still leading donkeys and goats in places where modern commerce is carried on.

I didn't want to go into the Holocaust Museum again, too much of an emotional strain. I stayed outside while the rest of the group went in. I quite enjoyed staying in the kibbutz again. Some of the group enjoyed riding on camels. I went back to the Wailing Wall again, a very interesting place. So many different faiths gathering there and I imagine from all over the world.

When our coach stopped anywhere there always seemed to be vendors around hoping you'd buy their scarves, postcards, necklaces, or whatever. They made quite a bit of money from the tourists. One stop we made for lunch, an outdoor tea garden, there were peacocks on the vacant tables hoping something had been left for them.

The guide explained that Israelis built their houses of material indigenous to that area and that many of the homes were built of a white stone.

Sometimes as I walked where olive trees grew, the ground underneath my feet would be carpeted with ripe, black olives and I couldn't help thinking, if they were harvested they could surely turn them into salad olives or olive oil instead of letting them go to waste.

By my last day our group had dwindled to three; a photographer and his wife from Montreal and myself being driven around Israel in a Mercedes. We had to be at the airport four hours before departure and again security was very tight at Ben Gurion Airport.

I am glad that I went again to Israel and did what I wanted to, observe more of the every day life there. Allan and Christopher were happy to see that I made it safely home. I told them about the chap in Toronto whose luggage passed by him on a carousel and he came out with an, "Oh, sh...," such a very human reaction!

I've done quite a bit of travelling alone and I must say fellow travellers have always been very helpful to me and there always seems to be someone there when needed. It may be because of my diminutive size.

As soon as I got back, Allan told me there was a note from our agent advertising a special cruise to Alaska on the Inside Passage and he said he would like to go, so we decided to talk more about that the next day. I was certainly glad that he was feeling up to it. We would have to make special arrangements for taking the oxygen along on both the airplane and the cruise ship.

There was, as always, quite a bit of fun in planning the journey as there was in taking one. Most of the time one liked to have casual, comfortable clothes and shoes, but it was always a good idea to pack one posh frock, no matter what kind of junket you took. And the men should plan to have something that looked dressy and a tie to go with it. I always packed a little at a time, doing it all at once was often overwhelming.

Allan was getting a little excited. He'd never been on a cruise before, although he sailed overseas to England during the war on a ship called the *Sumaria*. Booking so far in advance, I hoped that he would still feel like taking the trip when it was time to go.

Christopher drove us to Kelowna where we took the plane to Vancouver. Goodbyes were always sad, even though for a short time.

Janine met us at Vancouver to see us off on the next stage of our trip. And Janine, being Janine, was tearful on those occasions and as always she loaded us down with little gifts for the journey. She stayed with us in Canada Place while we waited for a long time to board the ship, but visiting with Janine made the time more pleasant.

We boarded the *Nieuw Amsterdam*, a lovely ship from the Holland-America line and there was a 'welcome aboard' party for us. The party was a very jolly affair and everyone seemed happy and friendly. There were flowers in the cabin to welcome us, a bottle of wine and a basket of fruit. At the time I rather imagined that that cruise would be *the* highlight of 1992. There were many thoughtful gifts in the cabin welcoming us aboard accompanied by a card of welcome from the BCAA and there were quite a few other gifts from them also during the cruise. With our tickets we had been given a large, bright red, carryall. It had the BCAA logo on it and I do think it may have said, *The President's Cruise*. Each passenger received a very smart looking album for snaps and memorabilia, also a red cape and a bright red umbrella with the BCAA logo on it, a pair of Bushnell binoculars and a clock that could tell you the time in most time zones of the world. And sometime on the cruise we were given a stuffed whale saying, 'We hope you're having a whale of a time'.

Although Allan couldn't join in a lot of the activities, he really did enjoy looking out of the windows in the lounge watching the sea and we did see some whales. The scenery going through the Inside Passage was breathtaking. Allan enjoyed the nightly live shows or sometimes he would watch a movie, and there was an art show. He liked to meet new friends and have a coffee or a cup of tea with them, so he never felt left out if I went ashore at the different ports; Kelchikan, Sitka, Juno, or if I was in the exercise room, or taking part in the line dancing.

On the *Nieuw Amsterdam*, as it was on the *Star Dancer*, the other cruise ship I was on a few years ago, our beds were turned down at night and there were two *Sweet Dreams* chocolates on each pillow. I think this particular brand is sold exclusively to cruise ship lines, for I've never seen them in stores.

I went once to the pool on the ship and Allan and I went to Mass most every day. He came with me one time to play the one-arm bandits in the casino and never played more than five dollars, but my problem was, I could never get rid of it in time to see the evening show.

At meal times Allan enjoyed the ice carvings, as did I. I think they played a *Radetsky March* while the chefs marched around the dining room with the baked Alaska's. There were occasions when they had ethnic dinners. The men were given a little black Dutch cap for Holland night, and the ladies a little white milk-maid hat. The food on board was perfectly wonderful. If I could find one fault, it would be to say that there was much too much food, especially when so many people in the world are starving. Maybe I shouldn't take this view, but certainly one could make a beast of themselves if they so desired.

We were very impressed with the shows the Indonesian and Filipino members of the crew staged. The Indonesians had an instrument they called an angklung. Each angklung only played one note, so it took many of these instruments to form their orchestra. I must say they made a very effective sound, and of course, we liked it when they played, *O Canada*. They tried to cover many national anthems. The Indonesians and the Filipinos who took part in these shows gave up their own time to rehearse and get things ready. This was only a seven day cruise, but we did seem to pack a lot into those seven days, and I was so glad that Allan did enjoy it and wasn't tired out by the whole thing.

On our return to Vancouver, Janine was there to meet us at Canada Place and we stayed overnight with her before flying back to Kelowna where Christopher met us with Bobbie. Christopher had taken care of everything pretty well while we were away. He had a nice dinner waiting for us and we told him of our adventures of the past week.

* * *

Timmie surprised us when he brought Patricia to meet us, for we had no forewarning that they were making plans to get married early the following year. A few weeks after that Timmie brought Patricia out again with her mother, a very pleasant person, and they stayed in the cabin. They talked about arrangements for the wedding and that Christopher would be Timmie's best man. Timmie and Patricia did a very good job planning the reception and the wedding invitations were so attractive and different. Not to be left out of the plans entirely, we helped a little with the financing.

We drove to Calgary for Timmie's wedding and the weather, to say the least, was brisk on the 13th of February. Patricia looked lovely in a white gown with a Juliet cap veil, carrying a bouquet of red and white roses. Her bridal attendant, Dalene, wore a red satin suit and carried a white posy. The boys were very nicely dressed in their navy blue suits, white shirts, red ties and red pocket-handkerchiefs. Timmie, Christopher, (Don, a family friend of Patricia's, took care of the usher's duties) wore red boutonnieres, Allan had a white one, and I had a red and white corsage. Father Cooney gave a moving service.

We talked briefly to Marie and Sheila, Allan's cousins, outside the church and though they were invited to the reception, they didn't attend. Auntie Lil was there, as were Cyril and Walter, Allan's uncles. Walter gave us some anxious moments when his crutches almost let him down on the ice around the reception hall. It was one of the nicer wedding reception dinners we had been to, and the music they had chosen throughout the ceremony was most inspiring.

Victor, Timmie's school friend, came all the way from Ontario to attend the wedding. Muff-Anne and Peter came with Megan and Katie. Janine and Paddie were there accompanied by a friend of his.

It was nice to see Jean, Patricia's mother again. This was the second time we had met Theresa, Patricia's sister who did a reading at the Mass. Her two children, whom we had never met before, were with her, Laura Jean and Eric. Nancy, Patricia's other sister seemed to be a very content person, even though she was in a wheelchair.

Theresa did a marvellous job of making the centre

Timmie and Patricia's wedding in Calgary, February 13, 1993.

Timmie with his firstborn, Joshua Allan.

pieces for the table decorations. To this day, years later, I still have mine, none the worse for wear. We stayed a few days in Calgary before returning to Vernon.

* * *

I spent a couple of weeks in England that year visiting Mary, Jack, Nan, and Mary and George. Steven and Martin were there for tea one day and that was nice. I went up to London to visit Louisa and Anna Marie and Johnny Jr.

We were at Windsor Castle again and went to some quaint little villages that hadn't changed in a hundred years. Jack made a great tour guide. He related so much of the history of the places in detail and made it so interesting. If we were out walking and passed rest rooms he had the most gentlemanly way of asking if you needed to use them. He would say, *"Are you comfortable dear?"* A lot more polite than saying, *"Do you have to go?"*

In one of those quaint little villages we saw some Clydesdales, those gentle, patient, beautiful workhorses I remember from my childhood. They used to pull the milk carts, coal carts and the garbage carts. They also pulled the barges walking along the canals and, of course, the gypsy caravan we lived in for a while. Sadly, these noble beasts are fast disappearing although many years ago they were so indispensable to the farmers. And we mustn't forget how much work they did for the breweries of Olde England.

Every time I stayed with Mary and Jack, we never missed a market day in Hemel Hempstead. Market days were always fun days. Though it was still quite early in the year, the weather was pretty fair.

In front of the map of Onjuko.

On the left Kiyoto, my friend Sakae whom I met in Israel,
and her daughter Atsuko.

Chapter 17

Land of the Rising Sun

When a letter arrived from Sakae in Japan, a friend whom I had met in Israel, asking me to come visit them, Allan thought it was a wonderful opportunity to see Japan, and said, "She has asked you quite a few times to go to Japan, so she really does mean it. It's not just something she said when the two of you met, while you were in Israel."

So I made arrangements to go later in the year and that was a memorable trip. Sakae met me at Narita Airport with her friend Kiyoto. They were holding up two large cards that read, 'Welcome Jacqueline Dahm'. The first thing Sakae said after the greeting was, "I hope you don't mind I bring my friend Kiyoto, she like to meet you." I told her I was quite delighted and when we got to Sakae's house there was a welcome meal awaiting.

Kiyoto stayed 'til Sakae's husband Siyouhie came home. He was working an evening shift, just two or three hours. He didn't have much English but he surely made up for it in the warmth of his greeting. He said as he extended both hands, "I very happy meet you," and took both my hands in his, such a nice man and such a nice couple. During my time with them Siyouhie would call me to come and watch the big Sumo wrestlers on the television. It was great fun to watch those big men flopping one another all over the ring. I took them a video of British Columbia and they just loved it.

They took me to beautiful Japanese gardens and to ancient temples and we had tea in a Japanese teahouse. While I was there, there was a special festive day when people dressed in their native costumes. It was most colourful and the children did look so cute. I saw a few groups of school children and they were all in uniform. I wondered if all school children in Japan wear uniforms.

We went to a Japanese bath-house and I chose to wear my swimsuit. We saw a play with kabuki actors and that was certainly different. Kabuki theatre began at the start of the 16th century, developed during the Edo Period when it was cultivated by merchants. Kabuki began as a means of expression for the commoner and all roles have always been performed by men.

I went to Sakae's church with her and afterwards we had coffee with the minister and two or three of Sakae's friends.

Kiyoto, Sakae's friend, and her husband had a little cottage right near the ocean and we stayed there for two days. There was Kiyoto, Sakae, one of her daughters, Atsuko, and myself. We went on one of those water busses that take people around for a turn on the water for an hour or so and that was quite bracing. We went to an aqua museum and strolled along the beaches.

On a bus tour of Tokyo, we went to a place where they process pearls, our tickets went into a draw for a pearl, but we weren't lucky. We went to a fair, quite similar to the fairs we have here in the West.

I liked the department store Justco, very much like our department stores here in Canada. Sometimes I would go there on my own to buy things for friends and family back in Canada. One particular day I think Sakae and Siyouhie may have been worried about me for Sakae sent Siyouhie to look for me in the store. He found me at the candy counter as I thought it would be nice to take some back to the house. They had bags you filled yourself for so many yen and Siyouhie said, "No enough, put more." So he filled the bags to the brim. I hadn't wanted to do that because I thought it might seem gross.

I must tell you something of the people of Japan, they were all so very courteous and kind. Atsuko was the first of Sakae and Siyouhie's daughters I met and she brought me a gift of wonderfully fragrant soap. Another daughter, Satchiko, came with her two little boys, one was four and one was eighteen months. She had a three-hour train journey and I thought it very nice that she made the effort.

Satchiko gave me a nice little ornament and really it was a bit embarrassing when everyone gave you presents, but that was the custom in Japan, everyone who met you, gave you a gift. Sakae gave me a kimono that had belonged to her grandmother.

A minister lady came to meet me and stayed in the house a couple of days; she brought me some warm mittens because she knew Canada was cold. The minister lady took us all out to an Italian restaurant and we made quite a large party, there were ten of us. The restaurant was quite near to Sakae's and Siyouhie's house, so we walked there.

Sakae told me that during the Second World War the Americans referred to Japanese houses as rabbit hutches. I would say Sakae's house was a lot more than a rabbit hutch. Ten of us lived in it at one time and we all slept quite comfortably!

Sakae's garden, though very small, was nicely kept. Everyone in Japan appeared to have a persimmon tree in their garden.

We went to see the Reverend Tsuda off at Narita Airport. He was going to Africa to minister to the people. Sakae was with Reverend Tsuda's group in Israel when we had met all those years before. You could say that he was instrumental in starting the friendship between Sakae and myself. Before leaving Narita he gave me a folding picture of various scenes in Japan and also showed me a picture that he had taken of me in Israel when we first met. He kept it in his wallet. I thought that was rather nice.

My last day in Japan, Sakae wanted me to show her some of the dishes we make in Canada. We only cooked two things but I left her with a Canadian recipe book, which pleased her.

The following day we readied ourselves to go to the airport which was quite near Sakae's house. Sakae and Siyouhie did not have a car. Siyouhie rode a bike back and forth to his job and short distances around Chibaken. Their daughter, Atsuko, drove us on longer journeys.

We walked to the airport and Siyouhie carried my

suitcase. I just had the one for I don't like being overburdened with luggage. There were many other gifts that Sakae and her husband wanted to give me but there was no more room in my suitcase. They told me they would keep them until I came the next time. Kiyoto, Satchiko and her little boys, and the minister lady also came to the airport. Before I boarded the plane Sakae said, "The last thing we give you is our heart," and I had to blink the tears away. Everyone there was so very kind to me.

* * *

1993 was almost over. There were still a few nice days when we sat on the lawn and watched the ducks and the geese on the water. Of course, the goose dog Bobbie wouldn't allow them to land on the lawn or the beach. He'd be after them like a shot. For that was his job, to chase the geese off the lawn and the beach, and he did it very well for nine years.

I remember on one occasion he picked up a little gosling. Christopher told him to "drop it," and he did. The gosling was very frightened, so we took it into the house and put it in a box with some soft cloth and bits of bread wondering if it would survive. In the morning it was peeping and exploring the laundry room. We took recently named *Gabriel Gosling* to the water where his mother was swimming to shore with his siblings and the family was reunited.

Allan still managed a little fishing and the weather was still kind enough to have a coffee on the patio in the evening and I managed to tidy up my little garden areas. Allan was still enjoying his game shows on TV and doing his crosswords. So all in all it had been a pretty good year.

Christmas
by *Muff-Anne York-Hayley*

I find myself
in this season to be jolly
manic-depressive
by its maudlin, mawkish magic.

The only thing
that saved me from
having a
nervous breakdown today
was:
fourteen cups of coffee
two packages of cigarettes
five va-li-ums
and a partridge in a
pear tree ...

'Tis the season
to be jolly.
Yes,
jolly well broke.

I am the ghost of Christmas past.
Please remit $789.53
on this truant account
immediately
or we will be forced
to turn it over
to a collection agency.

It started off
with Great Expectations
leveled off for a period
at A Christmas Carol
and wound up with
A Bleak House.
Now isn't that the Dickens.

Christmas was spent
in more ways than one
physically, mentally and monetarily.

Christmas is
carols and stockings
trees and plum puddings,
family and friends
together,
all enjoying the savory aroma
as the turkey roasts
in the microwave oven
for half an hour.

All is calm
but not very bright,
the city just cut off
my utilities.

It is a good thing
that Mary and Joseph
departed for Bethlehem
when they did.
Today the whole
venture would
set them back
about $5200.00 cash,
but then
there's always Chargex.

Forget the silver bells.
I'll take mine
in 24 carat gold.

The party was a hit
until my friend
burst out with
don we now
our gay apparel
and was asked to leave.

Oh, ho, the Christmas goose.

The mistletoe
caused much controversy
when Joseph and Michael
upheld the tradition.

Daughter Janine, myself and a young Dutch hostess
From the M.S. Statendam.

Breathtaking scenery on the Alaska cruise.

Chapter 18

Travel Logs

1994 - Dianne, our travel agent, sent us a flyer about an eight day Caribbean cruise. Allan said he would like to go on that cruise for he did enjoy the Alaska cruise. He said he really felt up to it. So we made all the arrangements and soon we were on our way to the Caribbean. Janine again met us at Vancouver Airport and waited with us in Canada Place 'til we boarded the ship, *S.S. Rotterdam.* We sat with Veronica and Doris, who lived in our area, at the 'Welcome Aboard' party, a light and happy affair. It was pleasant to meet two ladies from nearby. Veronica was a writer and Doris ran a care home.

There is something about cruises that brings out the best in people. The people at our dining table were friendly and everywhere we went, there was always someone ready for a little chat. I think the *Rotterdam* may have been a little bigger than the *Amsterdam,* certainly newer than the *Amsterdam.* We had a very nice outside cabin.

Allan had brought along his big book of crosswords but I don't think he got too many of them done for he spent a lot of time making new friends. I was very glad of this and didn't feel sad when I was taking part in some activity where he couldn't join in. He made friends with the priest on board. He met a couple of chaps who'd been in the army at the same time that he was, and they had also been in England.

Allan and I went to the movie, *Fried Green Tomatoes,* and to the wine tasting, the art showing, and he did enjoy the evening show and the presentations of the Indonesians and the Filipinos. Allan made a couple of bets on the horse racing although they weren't real horses. We had tea with Veronica and Doris a couple of times.

Passengers on a cruise ship are totally spoiled when it comes to food, almost any time of the day or night there is something to tempt the appetite. We didn't always go to the dining room; we'd have breakfast or lunch in the Lido room or on the barbecue deck, which were quite popular places. Allan was often apologetic. I remember him saying to me, "Do you think I might just have some melons please?" I felt so sad for him I could have cried. I knew that he was feeling bad because he couldn't do this simple thing for himself.

"You must have a little more than that," I said.

"I'm not very hungry," he replied. And that was that.

Sometimes he'd really fancy a sundae and I'd ask him, "What would you like on it?"

And he'd reply, "Anything you would like to put on it."

Allan especially enjoyed tea time when we met in the lounge and compared notes on what we had both been doing while we were apart.

One of us would invariably ask, "Have you seen Quilp today?" A name we had dubbed a passenger because of his astonishing resemblance to that character in Dickens' *The Old Curiosity Shop*. Quilp was always unexpectedly popping up in the strangest places around the ship.

I went once to the *Legs, Bums and Tums o' Fun* exercise group. I presented a reading of *My Financial Career* by Stephen Leacock on amateur talent night. I've always liked that piece because it is very funny and it's rather sad too. The idiocy of it probably appeals to me so much because of being in similar situations. I enjoyed playing the one-armed bandits again, knowing full well I could never be a big-time gambler.

I went ashore at the ports of call with some of the other passengers hoping to find something new and different to take back to family and friends in Canada. I always told myself, "*I wont' fall into tourists traps and get caught in those nasty nets, baited for the frantic tourist like me who is in feverish haste, who just has to get something for this one and that one, and mustn't forget Aunt Mary either, and I should get something for Charlie.*" All this mental torture we put ourselves through because we thought it absolutely necessary to bring back souvenirs to show where we've been, and really, did it matter that much? Maybe we did it because we didn't want to appear uncaring and selfish, or cheap? For me it was absolute mental agony because I hate and detest shopping with a terrible vengeance, even if I was shopping for diamonds and a fur coat for myself! And I always waited for the last port of call to do the dastardly deed.

It was good to see Allan perk up a bit and enjoy the break meeting lots of new people, but he was glad to be home again and so was I.

* * *

I took Janine on the Inside Passage cruise to Alaska and she was delighted with everything. I'd say she enjoyed those few days to the fullest and we were able to do lots of things together including line dancing and exercises. Janine loved the nightly shows, and we played Charades, and went to the casino.

The cruise ship was the *Statendam*, another of the Holland-America line's big ships. Their cruise ships all follow a similar format.

On that cruise we experienced more than a gentle rocking, and carrying our trays to the table from the self-serve areas was quite a balancing feat. It was announced that seasickness tablets were available at the nursing station; fortunately, neither Janine nor I had to avail ourselves of them.

It rained heavily when we went ashore in Juno, so we were glad of the umbrellas and rain capes we had been gifted on the previous cruise to Alaska. In Sitka we saw the Russian Dancers, they put on a very merry show that everyone seemed to enjoy.

Sitting at our table in the dining room was a doctor and his mother. He explained to us that it was payback time as his mother had paid his way through medical school and, therefore, he was taking her on this cruise. He said he preferred to eat in the Lido room or the more casual areas and wondered if I would go with him. I said I would, but Janine seemed to be quite disappointed because she liked to get dressed up, and she liked the idea of being served. Well it *was* nice, so I didn't go with James, the good doctor, to the more casual areas to eat.

Something I noticed in Alaska, the air was wonderfully clean. Janine and I did quite a bit of walking around the upper decks so we got our exercise and the air was very bracing.

* * *

Summer 1995 – The early event of that year was the birth of Timmie's son, Joshua Allan, on June the second.

We had been married forty-nine years, anniversary time. Timmie and Patricia came out from Calgary with Amy, a collie-cross, a beautiful animal; and stayed in the cabin. Timmie wrote a very moving poem for the anniversary. Even now when I read it, I have to blink away the tears. Timmie prepared a wonderful dinner, he is a good cook. It would have been nice if Muff-Anne and Peter and the girls, and Janine and Paddie had been there, but they were all too far away. Del and Bob, neighbours at the cabin, gave us a bottle of champagne. Timmie saw to the cake, but I don't think he made it, and there were flowers. July 27th, 1995, went into the treasure book of happy memories.

* * *

I took Janine on a short Mexican cruise that year, much the same as the cruise I took years ago. We were rather disappointed with the cruise. We thought the hostess assigned to the cruise could have been a lot more accommodating, but we did have lots of fun anyway.

On our return while waiting to disembark we heard someone in a nearby group say, "At least we got rid of the whistler." I guess 'the whistler' was some passenger who annoyed him by continuous whistling - one of those minor irritations that happened in daily living that gave cause for annoyance. I'm sure we're all familiar with these little, niggling, annoyances and surely we should all be more tolerant, for it is truly not worth getting distressed. And don't we all have little traits or habits that irritate others?

* * *

The owners of the house in Maple Ridge where Janine was renting a suite unexpectedly sold their house. Janine phoned upset and not knowing what to do. We suggested she come and live in the cabin until she found something more permanent. That was eight years ago and she is still there.

In order to make room for Janine's furniture, Timmie took the furniture and "stuff" from the cabin to Calgary as his house had room for it.

* * *

1996 - Allan I had been married fifty years. Our children and grandchildren planned a very special Golden Wedding Anniversary. The invitations were very beautiful. The tea reception was held at the *Tuck Inn* in Vernon. They thought it would be best to have a tea rather than a dinner because the event would not be as tiring for Allan.

A delightful tea it was, a variety of sandwiches and all kinds of dainties, a beautiful cake with real flowers on it. I'm pretty sure Muff-Anne made the cake. Oh yes, and there was champagne.

They did a wonderful job making everything go so smoothly. It just couldn't have been nicer. Helen and Jack Ward, cousins of Gram, came from Kaslo, quite a way from here. It was good to see them again as we hadn't seen them for a number of years. Bertha and Leo came from Kelowna and it was nice to be with them again. Heather was there, a friend I helped in the kindergarten. Brenda came, another friend from school. Alma and Evelyn were there, friends from the United Choir.

Margaret Cox, a one-time neighbour at the lake was with us, too.

I almost forgot to mention Dorothy McCorquadale from East Vernon was there, Corkie's Dorothy. Chiyo and her friend Ron, brought Mamma. Chiyo is Jimmie's sister. I'm sure I've mentioned Jimmie before, he was my neighbour at the lake. He used to call me his second mum.

Not a large gathering, for many of our friends we left behind in Calgary. Others lived too far away to come, and still others are no longer with us. It was an occasion well worth remembering, and our children and grandchildren planned everything to run along happily.

Everyone would have been happier to see Allan in better health and not having to take the oxygen tank everywhere he went. But I'm sure he was pleased with the gathering. It was the biggest event of '96.

* * *

Later that year I took my first trip to Ireland, the land of my ancestors, the O'Neill's. I was quite delighted with the country and it's people. Of both, I would have to say, quite charming.

We toured Ireland by coach. Though the tour wasn't long, we did see a lot in a very short time, Waterford, the factory where the world famous crystal is made and Avoca where *Ballykissangel* was filmed. Most of our group kissed the *Blarney Stone*, making sure to have the picture to prove it.

We were taken to a peat bog. Peat is cut from the ground much the same as turf would be cut. We found tiny cottages heated by peat fires and perhaps the cooking was done on these fires for there was no other source of energy evident for this purpose. I don't know if these little cottages are still in use today, but they probably were in the early 1900's and maybe a little later than that. One we went into had a little furniture therein. There was a double bed and a chair beside it. A curtain that could be drawn across for privacy. A rough table with a couple of chairs. A big black kettle on the fire. An old-fashioned jug and basin on what

Muff-Anne warming up in front of a peat fire in Ireland.

Muff-Anne overlooking the cliffs at Moher.

looked like an old packing case, a few rough shelves on the wall. Oh yes, there was a chamber pot peeking out from under the bed.

These would have been the humble dwellings that the very poor rented from rich, English land owners. I think most of the people in these cottages lived off the land and they may have had a few chickens. The owners kept an agent in Ireland to look after their interests and to collect the rents. Of course, the agents were properly housed with all the conveniences of that time. No humble dwellings for them.

History tells us that many of these English land owners gave instructions to their agents to turn out these poor downtrodden people and burn the cottages to the ground if they didn't pay their rents. I would hope there might have been land owners who showed more kindness to their fellow man.

It was fun going into an Irish pub and I think most of the people in our group had a taste of real Irish Guinness and quite liked it. A singer in the pub asked me to sing along with him. I did and that was fun too.

In front of Christys Pub October 1996.

We were entertained by Irish dancers in the hotel where we stayed and they were very good. Another evening at dinner we listened to a harpist and her music was very moving.

We were in Trinity College in Dublin where I was told, many years ago, my Grandfather had taught. When I asked one of the guides in the college where to find some history on the O'Neill's, he told me without flinching, "Sure, and we hung them all." He *was* being facetious.

When we visited a very old churchyard I found a headstone of an O'Neill and I'm sure he would have been one of my ancestors.

On one of the main streets in Dublin we viewed the very large and imposing statue of Charles Parnell, the Irish nationalist politician. He was quite a controversial figure. Born in the mid 1800's, in 1881 he organized an agrarian boycott and stopped all business in the House of Commons, until Gladstone passed the Irish Land Act. His influence of the Home Rule movement waned in 1887 when he was unjustly accused of political murders. And in 1889 when he was named as correspondent in a divorce suit.

In the dining room of the hotel where we were staying, I asked two people who were seated at a table for four, if anyone else would be joining them, and the woman replied, "You are."

We spent quite a bit of time together on the tour. Michael told me that his mother, Marion, was taking him on this tour, for he was dying of Aids. He had less than two years to live and this was the third such trip she had taken him on. We kept in touch, and when he died, his mother wrote and told me that getting rid of all his personal belongings was the hardest thing she'd ever done. I was very sad when he died. He was only thirty-three, but I believed that he enjoyed the land of his forefathers. And his mother, good soul that she was, was making sure he got the most from the time left to him.

Marion and Michael and I did our best to avoid a certain lady in the group. For whenever she managed to grab an ear, she would tell you of her trials and problems. On one such occasion we were having tea in a bright little spot and she came and sat with us, there was nowhere to hide so we couldn't avoid her. She was moaning to us how ungrateful her children were. And Marion said, "All children are ungrateful, they're supposed to be, aren't they Jackie?" I smiled and nodded agreement.

And I was reminded at that point of something many

years before, when my sister's son, David, was giving her a hard time and I told him, "You should be grateful to your mum."

At that time we just had the two little girls and he asked me, "Are your girls grateful?"

I told him, "Hmmm, sometimes." I was quite amused by his thinking.

I must say, our guide Maggie, made the tour fun and interesting. She played audio tapes along the way, some lovely Irish music and quite a bit of Irish humour and everyone seemed to enjoy them. Maggie had us writing limericks and I won the prize, a book of humour by Irish comedian, Hal Roach. I'm sure there was a movie producer or director many years ago whose name was Hal Roach.

We were in an old pub called *Dirty Nelly's*. Maggie told us that at one time it had been owned by a lady called Nelly who wasn't the cleanest person. It was told about that she washed the drinking glasses in her bath water. This may have been one of those colourful stories that gets more colourful as the years go by, as it has with *Dirty Dick's* pub in London.

We passed the Kennedy estate. I didn't know whether any of the Kennedy family was still living there.

We heard a story about a Judge Lynch. His son was alleged to have killed a man. No one wanted to punish him, so the judge hanged his own son. And supposedly this is where the word 'lynching' comes from.

Muff-Anne feeding the Royal swans at Windsor, 1996.

Chapter 19

On The Move Again

Back to Canada - Allan seemed to be increasingly unhappy at the beach. He didn't like the 'Happy Hour' that seemed to occur at any time of the day. He didn't like strangers coming in and taking over, and not having the good sense to stay near the units of whomever they were visiting. And he did get dreadfully annoyed when anyone made use of our lawn furniture without even saying, "May I?"

I think the final straw came one Saturday afternoon when I was outside our unit on the lawn reading. A couple of young chaps were playing frisbee, jumping over the chaise where I was reading. They hit the bird feeder with the frisbee, and then hit me with the frisbee. Poor Allan was so distraught. He said, "I don't want to live here any more. I hate it here."

Shortly after that he looked in the real estate guide and found a place for sale a couple of blocks away. He told me to go and make an offer on the place. I said it was too late in the game to make a move. But he was so distressed, I did as he asked, but the place was sold. The realtor showed me another home (where I still live today) and I was pleased with the house and property. I brought Allan to see it but he was too sick to get out of the car. But when he was later able to see the house and property, he was satisfied. Facing another move again, I thought I would go out of my mind, but Janine and Christopher helped, and it went not too badly, except for getting stuff from the crawl space, hunched over like gnomes. I truly think if I had to move again, they would have to put me away.

That move was really worth all the work and the effort involved, to see Allan content and more relaxed. He liked the quiet of the area, with no passers-by peeking in windows. He loved watching the cattle grazing on the hill and watching the birds at the feeders. Christopher took him around the neighbourhood in the wheelchair so he met a few people further afield than our immediate area.

Allan never complained about his illness, but he did get very frustrated because 'he couldn't do anything'. In fact he didn't realize how many things he did do. He kept the books, wrote the cheques for the bills, prepared the veggies, did the folding, put the snaps and pictures in albums, and other odds and ends too numerous to mention. And he mended a few broken toys brought home from the kindergarten. He was the one who thought out the plan for the big sun room, which made a lovely addition, and the other improvements to the house.

1997 - Work was going steadily ahead on the sun room and the other improvements to the house. Allan was very interested in the work going on, watching progress and impatient for it all to be finished. When I looked back over the years and thought of all the homes we lived in, it was always Allan's ideas that made them more attractive and livable.

One thing Allan really liked to do was watering the flower beds and the veggie patch. I think this may have been therapy for him.

He was sent to one or two new doctors who promised wonderful things for him, but they didn't come to pass. One doctor even predicted fifty percent more lung capacity. He should never have said that, for our own doctor told us that the new procedure repairing the lungs was not for him. Allan's lungs were too far gone, and the oxygen only helped him use the meager lung capacity that he had. But, of course, he always had hopes that something could be done.

Throughout his illness he never lost his faith. He enjoyed his game shows, doing the crosswords, watching the birds and the cattle, and enjoyed his family. He didn't drive much any more, just occasionally. I remember one Valentine's Day he couldn't go to the shops, so he cut me Valentines from the paper. These sentiments are not to be found in too many people.

We made a few trips to the hospital that year. Allan had a slight stroke and we called the ambulance. They took him to the hospital and I followed by car. We spent hours there. The doctor wanted to keep him in for a few days to keep him under observation, but there was no way Allan would stay. He'd seen too much of hospitals and had a terrible aversion to them.

I had a very hard time persuading him to go to the hospital when he fell over Bobbie, our little dog. I wasn't sure if that had happened or whether he had had another small stroke. He didn't really remember he just said, "I think I fell over the dog." But I did get him to the hospital and the doctor found that he had broken his nose when he fell. We found that doctor to be warm and caring.

We made another trip to the hospital when our own doctor discovered Allan had a growth that had to be removed. Our doctor let me stay through the operation, but the nurses weren't pleased. It was the last we saw of the hospital for that year. But we were back and forth to the doctor's office at regular intervals.

The Vernon Health Unit was helpful. They sent care people out to check on Allan and the DVA said he was to have anything he needed to make things easier for him. They ordered a scooter for him, but he didn't take it. For, he said, if there were a problem with it, he would be helpless to do anything.

Our festive season was very low-key that year. There was just Allan and I, Janine and Christopher. It was just too much of an effort for Allan to socialize. His breathing was too difficult, so we kept any social activities outside of the immediate family to a minimum.

It meant a lot to him to go to one of the mission churches. I told him he shouldn't stand when the congregation did, just to remain seated through the whole service. I'm quite sure that a lot of his prayers were said for people who were worse off than he was, and I don't think he ever asked for anything for himself.

1998 - the sun room was finished. We added another

bathroom that had a jet tub. Took out one of the lower kitchen cabinets to make room for an upright freezer, removed the lower part of what the previous occupants called the pantry and installed a dishwasher there. Made a spot for the microwave. Changed some of the light fixtures and put more attractive ones in place.

Outside we dug out some of the superfluous junipers. I didn't know why anyone would want to plant junipers, they were not nice to work around as they scratched you to bits. Even in water-filled ditches some of them burned out, as if scorched by fire, or killed by chemicals. There were junipers at the front of the property and along the boulevard. There was a juniper bush in the backyard about ten feet tall. I would have liked to cut it down, so much dead in it, but many birds made their homes in it. Wherever the surplus junipers were removed we planted flowers.

Allan decided he would like to have a wrap-around verandah with a ramp and he talked it over with the chap who built the sun room and did the other improvements. I wondered if this might not be too ambitious a project right on the heels of having all the other work done.

I didn't do any travelling that year even though Allan said I should. I didn't want to leave Allan any more, even though Christopher and Janine were nearby. He was not doing well at all, and didn't have very many good days. Because of his illness, being so frustrated and railing against it, he did get very unreasonable, even over the smallest things. But he always felt bad afterwards and would always say, "Do you forgive me?"

Christopher still took him around the area in the wheelchair and he always enjoyed it. He was still doing his crosswords, watching the game shows. And Janine would visit once a week or so. Muff-Anne and Peter and the girls came for a visit and stayed a couple of days. Al, a friend from Calgary, paid us a visit. Allan was glad to see friends, but it really was an effort for him to talk. He was on oxygen all the time and there were too many visits to the doctor. I took it as a good sign that he was still interested in things, and sometimes miracles could happen.

Bertha and Leo had an anniversary celebration in Kelowna, but Allan was not up to going. I went with Janine. Christopher drove us there and picked us up afterwards. I think it was their sixtieth anniversary. When Janine and I were leaving, Leo Jr. took a floral arrangement from one of the tables and said, "This is for Allan," and I was very touched by it. He is a special person.

Allan Dahm at the camping ground in Banff, Alberta, July 1925.

Chapter 20

Suffering Ended

1999 - Life moved along at much the same pace as it had. One of the highlights for Allan continued when Christopher took him around the area in his wheelchair. On one of these little journeys, he became friendly with a neighbour lady and took her a stem, of what I call, wild delphiniums, a wild orchid coloured flower with a lovely fragrance.

On April 13th of that year, Jennifer Maria was born to Timmie and Patricia in Calgary. (A little sister for Joshua Allan, who was born June 2nd, 1995 and christened in St. Theresa's Church on Westside Road, one of the mission churches. Jean, Patricia's mother, was Joshua's godmother, and Christopher, his godfather. Timmie and Patricia and Joshua stayed with Jean in the cabin where we had a nice little celebration to mark the occasion. And I can boast, I was quite happy with the cake I made).

Just a few weeks after Jennifer Maria was born, she was christened at a church in Salmon Arm. Patricia's sister, Theresa, lived there with her two children, Laura Jean and Eric. Allan wasn't able to go to the christening. Christopher drove Janine and I there. Christopher was Jennifer's godfather and Theresa was Jennifer's godmother. Shortly before the christening, I was in the church lobby with Timmie and he introduced me to a chap who seemed happy-go-lucky, shall I say careless in his dress, whose old runners weren't laced up, and he didn't wear socks. I didn't quite get the name, and when he left us, I asked Timmie, "Who was that chap?" Timmie answered, "That's the priest who's going to christen Jennifer."

There was a christening cake and coffee and we stayed and took pictures. Afterwards Janine came home and had supper with us, and although Allan's appetite was not the best, he enjoyed what he ate. Later, Timmie and Patricia dropped in on their way back to Calgary and when Allan was holding Jennifer he said, "This is a perfect baby."

The Y2K hype that began at the start of the year was gaining momentum in some quarters and may have reached ridiculous proportions. Some people thought it might mean the end of the world, or at the very least, the end of all of humanity's power sources. Others thought it would spell disaster for the computer world. And it took me, computer illiterate that I am, quite a while before I knew that Y2K simply meant year 2000, and it wasn't some mysterious computer signal.

The media did little to alleviate the panic, indeed they added to it. The makers of generators did very well, and Allan, ever thoughtful of the family, decided that we should have a generator. Christopher took him to Armstrong where he made the deal entirely on his own.

No matter how he felt, Allan always phoned his brother on his birthday, and he never missed calling an uncle and a cousin, boyhood friends, those who grew up together, on *their* birthdays. They were all about the same age. Sometimes I would have to dial the numbers for him.

Bernie came from Ottawa and spent a few days with us that year. He was shocked at the change in Allan who had lost about fifty pounds since Bernie had last seen him. That was the last time Bernie was to see Allan alive.

In the middle of June, Allan had what I thought to be another small stroke. It lasted just seconds and I said he must go to the hospital. But, of course, he didn't want to go. Finally, he agreed to go and after waiting what seemed to be an eternity in the emergency, the doctor we saw there was very concerned and wanted to keep him in the hospital. I knew that Allan wouldn't agree to that so the doctor put him on heart pills as she couldn't insist that Allan stay in the hospital.

For a while he seemed to be doing a little better by taking the pills. He enjoyed the nice summer weather, and liked to sit outside and listen to the birds and watch them at the feeders.

On July the 8th, his brother's birthday, Allan phoned his brother to wish him a happy birthday and they had a nice chat. He ate a little lunch and for dinner I got take-out chicken. Allan couldn't eat all his chicken and he told Christopher in fun, "You can't eat that, I'm putting my name on it, and I'm going to have it for lunch tomorrow."

That day Janine came for a visit before going back to the cabin. I went to bed much earlier than Allan and Christopher, as they watched the news together, read for a while then turned out the light around 10:30.

I was just drifting off to sleep when Christopher burst into the room saying, "Something's happened to Dad." He had already called for an ambulance, and while waiting for it to arrive, he was on the phone to 911, and they were telling him how to administer artificial respiration.

Shock makes things appear rather hazy in one's mind, but I remember very clearly, when the ambulance people took Allan away, he was placed on the stretcher so that his head was hanging over the edge, unsupported, and moving around freely. A little more care should have been shown and a little more respect, for this was my husband, and they should have treated him with more dignity. I was quite hurt by their actions.

His spirit had left this place. They took him to the hospital and we knew what the doctor was going to tell us.

There was a very nice nun, a Sister Lucille at the hospital whom we had met before. I'm not quite sure how she came to be there, for as I said, shock makes the mind very hazy. She was saying prayers for Allan and trying to comfort us. It was one of those times that has such an unreal quality about it, where you might wake up and find its all been a very bad dream. I had probably asked the nursing staff to call a priest. The priest was away at that time and Sister Lucille was doing what she could in his absence.

Somehow, we managed to get through all of the things that needed to be done. Made arrangements for a Requiem Mass, met with the funeral directors, put announcements in the papers here in Vernon and in Calgary.

Soldier's Farewell
by *Janine Allison Dahm*

God's peace and love surround you now
In the grounds that saw the wars.
A soldier boy no longer, a soldier boy no more ...
The wars for you are over.
The battles now have ceased,
And you will have your glory,
In God's great heavenly feast ...
You will always be remembered,
As a man who gave his best,
To his country, as a soldier,
To his family, as a quest ...
So rest now, brave soldier,
So rest now, Father dear,
And ask our Heavenly Father,
To comfort our sad hearts here.

Made many phone calls and sent out thank you cards.
Afterwards, There was, of course, a lot of legal business that
needed attending. Allan had left a holograph will, which
was legal in Alberta but not in British Columbia; that had to
be looked after.

I suppose most people when they suffer a loss wish
they had done this or that differently. I found myself
thinking the same, but no one can ever go back.

Allan died on a Thursday. I was with him at the
doctor's on the previous Tuesday when he told the doctor, "I
would like to live another couple of years. I would like to
have an operation for this hernia I have." And the doctor
told him, "No one would operate on you, it would be too

244

risky." But I think Allan's attitude showed that he still hoped something could be done for him.

About ten days before he died, the priest told me he would come to see Allan in a couple of days, and when I told Allan he said, "I look forward to that." The priest never came, nor was there even a phone call from him or a visit to the family to say that he was sad that Allan had left us. And this was one priest that we counted as a friend who'd been with us for dinner on more than one occasion. We were very disappointed and hurt. But, he was only a man, full of frailties as with us all.

The Mass for Allan was on the 14th of July, his dad's birthday. Muff-Anne and Peter and the girls came from Stony Plain. Timmie and Patricia, Joshua and Jennifer came from Calgary. And Paddie came from Vancouver. Lorraine and Bernie came all the way from Ottawa where they had moved some time previously.

The priest who said the Mass for Allan had lived in Corsica, but he was a Canadian. He had an elderly mother in British Columbia and perhaps he had come to visit her and while here filled in wherever there was a need. He belonged to the Grey Friars Order. He gave a moving service, warm and sincere. There were kind neighbours providing food, one everyday thing that we didn't have to worry about.

One never forgets, especially when you've been together for nearly fifty-three years, but like it or not, one had to go forward and get on with the business of living. For quite a while I was barely getting through the days, but after time passed, it happened that I started to take a little interest in things again.

I have to say, Allan was the most generous person I have ever known, and all of our children say he was the best Dad.

I didn't know how I would feel about going back and helping in the kindergarten. I had been there many years and I quite enjoyed helping. I did go back in the fall of 1999.

It was on April 13 of that year 1999 that Timmie's little girl Jennifer Marie was born.

To Somebody Dear
by *Jacqueline O'Neill Dahm*

It's lonely here without you,
There's such an empty space,
And what I wouldn't give or do,
Just to see your face.

But I know this cannot be,
At least not yet awhile.
So till that day when we are free,
We must brave up and smile.

But still I can't help saying,
How I wish that you were here.
And I'll go on praying,
Till that day draws near.

You know I pray at 'let's pretend',
And fancy I can see you smile,
And that I'll see you Dearest Friend,
In a little while.

Will it be just by the pond?
While I am walking there?
Will someone wave a magic wand?
To reveal you standing there?

My friends Jack and Mary, my son Christopher,
Jack and Mary's granddaughter Louise,
their great-granddaughter Kate, and of course, me.

Jack and Jacqueline with Neptune himself.

Chapter 21

Life Goes On

The following year Christopher and I went to England and he really liked that country.

We stayed with Mary and Jack for a while. And Jack, wonderful guide that he was, took us to places of interest and told us some of their history. Stratford-on-Avon, the birthplace of Shakespeare, Banbury Cross where the lady with the rings on her fingers and the bells on her toes rode a white horse. We saw the Rock of Ages, made famous in the hymn.

In Wallingford, the little village where Jack was born, he took us in the church where he was baptized and sang as a choirboy. Wallingford was one of those quaint unchanged little villages that are dotted all over England. On the gable end of one of the shops there hung a pennyfarthing bicycle. I didn't know if they sold bicycles or not, but I'm quite sure they don't sell pennyfarthing bicycles.

We went down to Swindon to see Louise and family. Louise is Mary and Jack's granddaughter. We didn't go to Otford, Kent, this time, another quaint little village where my friend Nan used to live, but she had left this place for a better one.

We had a little visit and tea with Mary Bird, had tea in Brighton and spent a little time on the beach. Looked around the shops in *The Lanes*, and then took a train back to Victoria. We took a tube from Earl's Court, where we were staying and planned to go and see Louisa in the evening the next day.

Christopher was very fond of Cornish pasties and sausage rolls fresh from the bakery and still warm when you got them. So after doing London, the National Gallery, feeding pigeons in Trafalgar Square, Cornish pasties and sausage rolls was our supper along with some gooey things and very large coffees from MacDonalds. When we arrived at Louisa's, she had a mountain of sandwiches, a very large cake and wine and coffee and apologized all over the place that she hadn't had time to cook a proper dinner for us. Anna Marie and Johnny Jr. were there, and we hoped that they wouldn't notice that we didn't eat too much, but we had a lovely visit with them.

We went back to Mary and Jack's in Hemel Hempstead the next day and hired a car for Christopher was to drive us to Wales. Jack showed us the turnoff to take and Christopher did wonderfully well driving on the opposite side of the road, steering wheel on the other side, and in a strange country. He didn't mind it at all. My poor Allan hated driving in England, he couldn't get on to it at all, so mostly we took taxies and tubes.

We visited Cardiff and Porthcawl, where we stayed. We thought it a pretty place. It was on the Bristol Channel. Some days the water looked quite angry. We would have liked to stay there longer as there were some nice little shops in town. Anyone would think I liked shopping, but it's something that I would rather not do. We promised Mary and Jack we would be back on a certain day, so we had to leave. We spent a couple more days with Mary and Jack then returned home to Canada.

I haven't told you anything about the trip I made to Medjugorje some years ago; it was organized by a priest in the United States. There must have been about two hundred on that trip, a few Canadians, but the majority were Americans. Medjugorje is a little village in Yugoslavia where three young visionaries saw Our Lady. There were quite a few people in the village when I was there, and at that time it was under Communist rule, but I don't think it is any more.

The church there, although it was a fair size, was very plain, unlike so many churches one finds in Europe. And there were no tourist facilities as such. There was no hotel, and certainly no motels, so we were billeted in private homes, apartment buildings, or wherever there was an available room.

There was word going around that people had had their rosaries turned to gold, and of course, there never were any rosaries turned to gold. I don't think the good Lord would have been concerned with things like that. He'd be more concerned about the poverty in the world, the sickness in the world, and the wars in the world. And this turning rosaries to gold would only be in people's minds.

We were in Oberammergau and saw the *Live Passion* play. It is a tradition that those taking part in the play must be born in Oberammergau and there were no wigs or false beards worn. The actors must grow their own beards and grow their hair long, if the part calls for that.

When I said there were no tourist attractions that was not quite right. For enterprising people always abound wherever a chance of money could be made. There were little stalls, and little nooks and shops where you could get souvenirs from Medjugorje. I don't know what the population of Medjugorje would be without the tourists, it was just a village, but with the influx of people the church was overflowing and many sat outside on benches, with loudspeakers to hear the Mass. I noticed the soil in Medjugorje was very red, I suppose that would mean there was a lot of iron in the earth.

In Zagreb when I asked them at the desk at the hotel where we were staying, would they please put a call through for me to Canada, they were very brusque, not accommodating at all. We were also in Sarajevo briefly and spent a little time in Austria and Hungary.

It was on this trip that I met Genevieve, a nun from Orange, California, and we became quite friendly. We'd eat lunch, have tea, take a swim, and go for walks together.

She shared a room with another nun and it wasn't working out too well. The other nun, to say the least, was rather bossy and quite intimidated Genevieve, who was a gentle soul. Poor Genevieve would say, "I don't know why she can't stand me." And I told her, "There's nothing wrong with you, it's not your fault, maybe she doesn't like herself. She may be a nun but she's not much of a Christian."

Sister Genevieve from Orange County,
California, whom I met on my trip
to Medjugorje.

Genevieve and I thought we were quite enterprising if we found a place where tea was just one dollar American. I haven't heard from Genevieve for some time. She used to write quite regularly, so I do hope she is all right.

I realize that not everyone is familiar with the story of Medjugorje. The young visionaries were said to have seen Our Lady and she gave them messages.

* * *

End of the year 2000, and the world didn't come to an end and the computer world wasn't thrown into chaos. However, our family world was very much saddened by the loss of Allan, but we got on with the business of living and taking care of things that had to be done.

There have been special occasions that are very hazy in my memory such as the Christmas of '99. I think we probably spent it here, just the three of us, Janine, Christopher and myself. The time when Muff-Anne and Peter renewed their wedding vows twenty years after they married, that must have been in '99. I think it may have been in August, very soon after Allan left us. I know the ceremony wasn't in Stony Plain and I don't really remember where it was. I think for New Year's 2000 we were with Janine at the cabin, but as with all the special occasions, they were rather empty because Allan wasn't there.

Christopher had started working with *Precision Construction* in January of that year. He'd leave the house about 6:00 a.m. and return some time after 4:00 p.m. Quite long days for him. So it was just Bobbie and I at home.

I was still going to help at the kindergarten on Tuesdays. Janine would come and spend some time with Bobbie on that day so he wouldn't be too lonely. I would leave her a lunch and some treats for Bobbie. They'd share this time together and Janine would take Bobbie for a walk.

I think Bobbie enjoyed these Tuesday visits and they did come about quite by accident. Janine was in the neighbourhood one Tuesday, preparing to leave something at the door, but the door was open, so she just came in and shared some time with Bobbie. And I said that would be a good idea every week, because Bobbie did get lonely and Bobbie loved company. He was quite elderly, fourteen years old, but sometimes he still thought he was a puppie.

One little girl saw him waiting outside a store for Christopher and she said, "Look Mummie, an old puppie."

In April of that year Maggie married Jason. Harvey and Tony came out from Calgary and spent a couple of days with us. We took them to the *Allan Brooks Nature Centre* and they enjoyed it. We all had an evening with Janine at the cabin and she made a very nice dinner. I think they quite enjoyed their trips around *Crazy Henry's* and the *Welk Mart*, two stores that are really different and what you can't find in one, you're bound to find in the other. When you are in the *Welk Mart* you must tread very gingerly and keep your elbows tucked in. There are a lot of breakables and the aisles aren't that wide and notices everywhere, "You break, you buy." And when you are in *Crazy Henry's* you imagine you are back in time in an old fashioned trading post. They do have character, that's for sure.

After their visit Tony and Harvey went on to the coast where Joanne, Harvey's sister lives, and shortly after they left, events happened that took the lives of thousands and affected the whole world.

* * *

It was early morning September 11th. I was just emptying the dishwasher when Christopher came in. He had been watching television in the sun room and couldn't believe what he had seen. He saw the two towers on the *World Trade Building* topple. There were people running, screaming, crying in the streets. Police and firemen everywhere. Terror and chaos reigned supreme. Christopher said, that when he turned on the television he thought he was watching a science fiction movie. An American Airline flight with ninety-three people aboard, including eighty-two passengers, five of them hijackers, and nine flight attendants and two pilots were all killed as the

254

plane crashed into the north tower of the *World Trade Centre*. And sixty-five people, fifty-six passengers, including five hijackers, seven flight attendants and two pilots were all killed when a United Airlines flight crashed into the south tower of the *World Trade Centre*. And when an American Airlines flight #77 crashed into the Pentagon, sixty-four people were killed, fifty-eight passengers, including five hijackers, four flight attendants and two pilots. And when United Airlines flight #93 crashed in Pittsburgh, forty-four people were killed, including thirty-seven passengers, four of them hijackers, five flight attendants and two pilots. This last plane was to target Camp David, but missed.

The one behind all this mass murder and terrorism was Osama Binladen and the despicable deed was carried out by his henchmen. In one of his speeches, Binladen said God wanted him to do this - definitely not the thinking of a sane mind! Since that day, the world has never been the same. The worst of the consequences being, thousands killed, families' lives shattered, having to start again without loved ones, survivors who will carry the trauma of that day for the rest of their lives.

9/11 had consequences so far reaching we couldn't begin to imagine. Many firemen lost their lives that day and many policemen. Entire businesses were wiped out because everyone in them was killed. People were jumping out of windows on the ninetieth floor. Couples holding hands jumping out of windows.

Certainly 9/11 has gone down in history as the worst terror attack ever. And security has never been so tight, also vigilance all over the world, especially at airports. There are plans in the making for rebuilding the *World Trade Centre*, but they haven't gone forth yet, and I think the damage to the Pentagon has mostly been taken care of.

Today is this mad man still alive who caused such suffering and pain to so many? Some think he's hiding in another country other than his own. There are so many people whose shattered lives will never be the same and some who never can rebuild their lives because of this man of darkness and evil. The world was still reeling from these events for many months after.

(Just before this happened, Muff-Anne was travelling with a church group going to Cleveland and if they had been any later, they wouldn't have been allowed into the United States of America).

* * *

Jottings

In October, Janine met Dennis who became a very important part of her life. We first met Dennis at the cabin in the fall of 2001 when he and his mother spent Christmas with us, so there were five of us instead of three and time went by very pleasantly.

Maggie and Jason came for Thanksgiving, Kescia was there also, but she wasn't born until January the following year. Maggie, Muff-Anne's oldest daughter, was given up for adoption when she was born, for Muff-Anne was not married then, and thought this was the best and wisest thing to do. However, about twelve or thirteen years ago, each was looking for the other, and they found one another. Soon after that Allan and I, and the boys first met Maggie. Of course, I had seen her as a baby. Now I have six grandchildren and one great grandbaby. She's a dear little girl and when she was here, she squealed with delight at Bobbie and I was so afraid that he might have been grumpy with her, because he was very old, but he wasn't.

Muff-Anne and Peter and Megan from Stony Plain visited a few days and then they went to see Muff-Anne's new granddaughter. Muff-Anne helped me colour a lot of pictures for the kindergarten while she was here and also helped me with some of my mending and sewing. She's a lot better at it than I am and I know she doesn't get her sewing expertise from me.

Alice and Cec dropped in on their way home to Red Deer. They are long time friends from the Court House. I was so happy to see them.

Chiyo and I, and another friend Carol, went to Lake Chelan to do a little gambling, but I don't think Chiyo or I will be going to Lake Chelan again. We had to meet the bus at five in the morning and were on that bus for five hours. No, definitely we won't be going there again and there is a casino here in Vernon. Chiyo didn't take a lot of time off.

She was taking care of Jimmie her brother, my ex-neighbour at the lake. He had terminal cancer. She was also the caregiver for her elderly mother who died a few weeks after Allan.

The list of family and friends who have left this place of late, seems never ending. Don, Allan's best friend in the army has gone. Don, and his wife May, spent a happy Stampede week with us years ago in Calgary. Leo is no longer with us, nor is Nella, who was one of the first friends I made in Canada. The list seems to go on ad infinitum.

Janine and Dennis took me to a comedy at the Armstrong, *Caravan Theatre*. I don't remember the name of the play but it made a fun evening. One old chappie in the audience added to the humour of the evening when he turned his chair around to face the audience and said, "I have called this meeting because......." The reason he gave was drowned out by the laughter and giggling.

The Armstrong *Caravan Theatre* is an open-air theatre. It gives aspiring actors a chance to be part of their group. A P.S. here. One had to take their own lawn chairs or seating along.

It was also in Armstrong, Janine and Dennis took me to see the little donkeys. I love little donkeys. They seemed to tell us a secret, they know one of their little ancestors carried Mary many years ago.

On the 9th of September that year, Janine and Dennis invited us to a barbecue. We were almost ready to go when I discovered that the hot water tank was leaking. The plumber I use didn't work on Saturday. I phoned another and he did the work, but his bill was astronomical. I could tell you the whole story but I'm quite sure you would be absolutely bored silly.

I told my friend Heather, that that would be my last year helping in the kindergarten, for there were other things I would like to do, and one would be to finish this story. I'm not eighteen anymore and the years have a habit of dwindling.

At the end of September, little Bobbie wasn't doing very well. He wasn't eating properly and was very listless.

The vet gave us some medicine and he seemed to perk up a bit for a little while. About ten days before this we had been able to tempt him with some tuna fish, he ate the whole can. But that was the last thing he was to eat at home. We took him to the vet a couple of more times, the last nearing the end of October. They kept him in the hospital for four days.

Christopher was working during the day. I would go and see him in the mornings and he looked a very sad little dog. The vet told me that he was trying to tell me something. "He's very tired." He was fifteen and a half. I asked the vet, "Please try and make him better." He put him on heart pills, but they didn't help much and he ate very little while in the hospital.

On the 28th of October, Janine, Christopher and I went to the animal hospital and asked if we might bring Bobbie home for the evening. The vet said, "If you will bring him back in the morning, you may take him home."

He gave one bark going up the steps and wagged his tail once, went into the kitchen and laid down by the island. Christopher stayed up with him until five o'clock the next morning. When I got up at seven I checked on him, he was very cold. I don't know if he knew me or not. I told Christopher, "I am going to phone the vet and he will put him to sleep." That was such a sad day for us when we lost our little Bobbie; even the vet had tears in his eyes when he put him to sleep. I'm sure he was sad too.

Little Bobbie was laid to rest on October 29, 2002. Christopher made a resting place for him crying all the while and we said little prayers for him, sending him to doggie heaven. Now there are daisies, honeysuckle, marigolds and poppies and pansies covering his resting place.

We couldn't stand being in the house without Bobbie, so we went to the SPCA that October day and looked at all the animals there.

The vet had told us that the sooner you get a little puppy, getting into all kinds of mischief, the better. We brought home three month old Billie Boy, a Cocker-Cavalier cross. A dear little fellow. Believe me he couldn't find enough mischief to get into and he still does, but I don't think he's as bad as he was then.

Christopher's work with *Precision Construction*, ended at the end of October that year. Since then he has been doing quite a bit of graphic art and other artwork. He did a bit of volunteer work for a gallery here in town building shelves and stands for them and he is hoping one day to get a foot in the door in the art world.

Hilda, Dennis's mother, invited us for a lovely dinner in Armstrong. We didn't stay long because of Billie. We didn't know what mischief he'd be getting into. We put him in a bathroom, and the few times he'd been in there, he scratched much of the paint off the door. And when we came home he was crying piteously, and it was rather sad. It made us feel very mean to leave him.

Christmas season and Janine and I went to the Clarica *Clients Appreciation Night* at the Prestige Inn, quite a nice evening.

At Christmas, Dennis asked if he might see slides of when Janine was a little girl. And so we watched until the projector gave out. Later, when we tried to get it repaired, no one had ever heard of this relic from the dark ages. We phoned Calgary and Vancouver to see if anyone there knew if they were making Hanimex projectors any more. We drew a blank there also. We've got about 50,000 of these Hanimex slide wheels that will only fit a Hanimex projector. (Why can't the manufacturers of these things make all slide projectors and slide wheels friendly to one another universally? I know the answer to that one. It just wouldn't be as profitable, would it?) Anyway, Christopher with a bit of ingenuity was able to repair the very fragile plastic part, the lever to raise the slides to project them onto the screen which gets the most use of any other part of the projector. Goodness only knows why metal wasn't used on this part. Even a child would know that. Anyway, for now it is working as long as the operator tip-toes around it and handles it like eggshells.

We had New Year's at the cabin and that was a fun time. We played silly games with much giggling. Decorations inside and out were just lovely, and they did rate first prize for all over the cove. A cheery fire was blazing on the hearth. There were tasty things to eat and the welcome was warm. Dennis added to the chuckles of the evening blowing several noisemakers at once and the effect was very funny.

Christopher relaxing at the cabin.

2003 was welcomed in on a happy note by Billie Boy making himself quite at home, nibbling coffee table edges, scratching paint and weather-stripping off doors, five of them so far, chewing up slippers, photo albums, and my income tax receipts, that's just some of his mischief.

I was his mummie until he was six or seven months old, but because Christopher rough-housed with him, he slept on Christopher's bed and Christopher took him for walks. He bonded with Christopher and ignored me and I was quite sad.

So I told the family that I was going to get a little dog just for me and it was going to be a little girl and I would call her Dorothy Jane. I phoned around quite a bit, even as far as Vancouver to find a little girl Cavalier-King Charles. I finally found one in Kelowna. I learned quite a bit about her by phone before we left to get her. It was one bright Sunday in early February 2003. We brought home Dorothy Jane, a little Blenheim Cavalier-King Charles. She was four months old. Very dear and very adorable. Our vet told us they made wonderful little pets and that you couldn't choose a better breed and they have such sweet little faces.

I mentioned dear Billie Boy was a half Cavalier. I was hoping he would have looked more like a Cavalier than a Cocker Spaniel, but he was all Cocker Spaniel, except he had the lovely soft eyes of the Cavalier and a beautiful nature. We call him Gentle Billie. His mother, a Cocker Spaniel, was a lovely animal with a nature to go with it and this little boy certainly took after his mother. We never did see the father. Billie Boy and Dorothy Jane were quite happy to have one another as siblings and loved to play together.

* * *

Dorothy Jane, now nicknamed Dollie, has settled in well and seems to love her new home and her new brother. But there is a cloud on our little family and we mentioned our concerns to the vet telling that that if she moved too fast, she squeaked and that many times a day her head shakes, her back legs seem straddled, and she doesn't hold her tail right, and there have been a few occasions where she has fallen over.

The vet took x-rays and tests and I don't think even he is sure of what it is. He said it could be epilepsy, or it could be Multiple Sclerosis. I thought M.S. was just a disease that humans got. I didn't know animals could get it. If it is epilepsy, there are medications for this and she could live a perfectly normal, healthy and happy life. If it should be M.S., I think that is ongoing and progressive, but whatever it is, we'll do whatever we can for dear little Dollie.

The owner of the kennels she came from said if anything bad happened with her she would replace her with another little dog, but of course, she couldn't be replaced. Can you replace one of your children? Despite all of her symptoms she does seem a happy little thing. We'll take her back to the vet in a few days and see then what he has to say.

Whenever I sit down in the sun room, Billie Boy thinks it's time for him to come and sit with me, along with Dorothy Jane who always sits with me. And since we got Dorothy Jane, Billie still wants to share in my affections, and they're both with me in the evening when I watch an hour or so of television.

Billie is so much like Bobbie, but a lot more demonstrative. Bobbie's favourite person after Christopher was handyman Glen. He just loved Glen. Now and again through the day, Bobbie would check to see if I was still around. Guess he liked me a little bit! Billie's favourite person next to Christopher is Dennis. When he sees Dennis, he waits for him to sit down and jumps on his lap, and if Dennis is standing up he almost knocks him down.

Dear Billie, he's really quite big to be a lap dog, but he's so affectionate. I think he loves everybody, but our little Billie isn't the brightest star in the doggie world. I wonder if that's why he has a perpetual worried look. Sometimes we call him *Worried William*, as he often has the look of a worried lion cub.

It is now the end of June, 2003 is half over. In March the war in Iraq started. So much bloodshed, so much

*In the backyard with my friend Nora,
Dollie and Billie standing guard.*

*Way back in 1974 little Tommie came
into our lives, shown here protecting
one of his little feline friends.*

heartache, suffering, pain, and hunger. Now they are trying to rebuild the country, but still sporadic fighting goes on. All is far from being well in that country.

Canada is experiencing a SARS outbreak. It started in Asia taking many lives there. There is now Mad Cow disease, crippling the beef industry in Canada and bankrupting some of those who raise cattle. It will take many years to put the cattle industry back on its feet.

And there are so many places of unrest all over the world. What of Israel and Palestine. Are they never going to be at peace? And why can't the Catholics and Protestants in Ireland live in harmony? Maybe it is because, as I often say, we human beings are not very nice people.
Goodness only knows why the dear Lord died for us. Hoping maybe to help us to scorn the base side of our nature and lift us above ourselves to aspire to more noble things.

Even with all the frailties of humanity and putting aside my earlier remark, many dedicated, selfless beings do exist, giving time, talent and resources, making this old world a better place to live in.

Matthew's Song
by *Janine Allison Dahm*

I am the sun in morning,
I am the bird that sings,
I am the laughter of the brook,
For now I have my wings.

My place is now in heaven,
With our father here above,
Together with the angels,
I watch o'er you with love.

My life on earth was very good,
As earthly lives can go,
Our Father's house, is so much more,
Than you can ever know.

Please don't sing sad songs for me,
For we are not apart,
Just look into your quiet place,
I am there within your heart.

And please don't shed your tears for me,
For I am not afar,
Look into the sky at night,
I am the brightest star.

When the rain falls softly,
Listen to the rain,
You will hear me whisper,
I'll see you all again.

*On our trip to the Netherlands in 1997, Muff-Anne who took this picture
in Breda, exclaimed, "At last, Mummie has found
someone smaller than she!"*

ISBN 141204724-2